MW00344055

Concepts of International Relations, for Students and Other Smarties

Concepts of International Relations, for Students and Other Smarties is not a stereotypical textbook, but an instructive, entertaining, and motivating introduction to the field of International Relations (IR). Rather than relying on figures or tables, *Concepts of International Relations, for Students and Other Smarties* piques the reader's interest with a pithy narrative that presents apposite nutshell examples, stresses historical breaks, and throws in the odd pun to get the big picture across. While there are other brief, introductory IR titles, Iver Neumann's book remains fully within the academic genre, and is comparatively long on history. It is based on his repeatedly offered introductory lectures to first-year IR students and students from other disciplines looking for an overview course at the London School of Economics and Political Science.

With a relaxed lecturing style, this textbook introduces the long-term historical emergence of concepts such as the state (European), the state (global), empire, nonstate agents, foreign policy, the states system, nationalism, globalization, security, international society, great powers, diplomacy, war and peace, the balance of power, international law, power and sovereignty, intervention, gender, and class. It demonstrates how such phenomena have been understood in very different ways. First, the reader is alerted to how the use of concepts is an integral part of politics. Second, the reader is sensitized to how social change has worked in the past, and is working now. Third, the book demonstrates how historical and social context matters in ongoing international relations.

Iver B. Neumann is Director of Norwegian Social Research (NOVA). He was formerly the Montague Burton Professor of International Relations at the London School of Economics and Political Science.

Concepts of International Relations, for Students and Other Smarties

IVER B. NEUMANN

University of Michigan Press ✦ *Ann Arbor*

Copyright © 2019 by Iver B. Neumann
All rights reserved

This book may not be reproduced, in whole or in part, including illustrations, in any form (beyond that copying permitted by Sections 107 and 108 of the U.S. Copyright Law and except by reviewers for the public press), without written permission from the publisher.

Published in the United States of America by the
University of Michigan Press
Manufactured in the United States of America
Printed on acid-free paper
First published February 2019

A CIP catalog record for this book is available from the British Library.

Library of Congress Cataloging-in-Publication Data

Names: Neumann, Iver B., author.
Title: Concepts of international relations, for students and other smarties /
    Iver B. Neumann.
Description: Ann Arbor : University of Michigan Press, 2019. | Includes
    bibliographical references and index. |
Identifiers: LCCN 2018034878 (print) | LCCN 2019000953 (ebook) |
    ISBN 9780472124800 (E-book) | ISBN 9780472074075 (hardcover : alk. paper) |
    ISBN 9780472054077 (pbk. : alk. paper)
Subjects: LCSH: International relations—Textbooks. | International relations—
    Philosophy. | International relations—Social aspects.
Classification: LCC JZ1242 (ebook) | LCC JZ1242 .N48   2019 (print) |
    DDC 327—dc23
LC record available at https://lccn.loc.gov/2018034878

Cover photo courtesy of NASA.

To my students at the London School of Economics, 2012–2017:
never underestimate your own students.

"No, no! The adventures first," said the Gryphon in an impatient tone: "explanations take such a dreadful time."

LEWIS CARROLL

Preface

When I came to the London School of Economics in 2012 to take up my chair in International Relations (IR), my colleagues paid me the compliment of asking what I wanted to teach. I answered that I wanted to take on the introductory course for new undergraduates. A short silence followed. Given the cultural context, this amounted to a rather strong reaction. I must have confirmed their worst fears of what it would entail to hire a Norwegian. The done thing, I learned later, would have been for me to offer an introductory course for the doctoral students. I ended up doing that as well, but teaching IR 100 was still the high point of my London years.

The pedagogics of the thing were blatantly narcissistic. I asked myself how I myself would have liked to be inducted into IR when I was coming up. In the lingo, I made my own younger self my implied listener. I would have liked to be inducted into the social and political by way of the language that is used. As it happens, there exist Anglo-American (the Cambridge historians), French (poststructuralism), and German (conceptual history) approaches that look at how this works, so there was more than enough material to draw on. And so, while sitting on my commuting flight from Oslo to London Heathrow and from Heathrow to Holborn every Monday, I would sketch out on my iPad where different IR concepts come from, and how they are used today. Come a new academic year, I would flesh out last year's notes even more, until I found myself with something that began to look like a manuscript. I then hired my doctoral student Andreas Aagaard Nøhr to freshen it up, and showed individual chapters to sundry colleagues. My actual first-year listeners asked valuable questions. Emily Gloinson and Ellen Tveteraaas commented on the entire manuscript from a first-year IR student perspective. My students Bjørnar Sverdrup-Thygeson and Adrian Rogstad commented from a teaching assistant perspective. Thanks, all.

Contents

1 ✦ Introduction

> Only that which has no history can be defined.
>
> FRIEDRICH NIETZSCHE

The great scientists of the end of the 18th century were the last ones to roam across the entire spectrum of intellectual pursuits. During the 19th century, a new science of the social emerged. The great social scientists of the end of the 19th century covered all aspects of the social. The end of the 19th century and the beginning of the 20th also saw a certain specialization, however. Hiring patterns in universities and publishing patterns conspired to institutionalize new disciplines. Each new discipline congealed around a certain core object of study—sociology around society, political science around the state, economics around the economy, anthropology around what was not modern. International Relations, or IR, was the name given to social order among political units. We call it international *relations*,[1] as distinct from international politics, because politics is a concept that refers etymologically to what happens inside a *polis*. With two caveats, our subject matter is what happens between and not within political units, and so we talk about relations and not politics.

Now for the caveats. Beware, first, that International Relations (IR) is the study not only of the emergence of relations and patterns of relations between political units, but also of how one particular political unit conducts itself in relation to other units, that is, what we call foreign policy. To study IR is first and foremost to study structures. The study of foreign policy, on the other hand, is the study of agents: what states do and how people within them think. It follows that IR studies relations not only as such but also as these relations are planned, executed, and experienced by the agents that are party to those relations. We call this the study of foreign policy.

Beware, second, that International Relations is not only the study of relations between nations. It is not only the study of nations understood as peoples, and it is not only the study of nations understood as states—as when we speak about the institution of the United Nations and mean the united *states* of this world. It is the study of relations between (Lat. *inter*) *all* political units. We need a term for all different kinds of such political units. The term of choice is, I think, suggested by IR scholars Yale Ferguson and Richard Mansbach (1996, 34), who use the term *polity* and define polity as being a group of humans that has (a) a self-reflected identity or "we-ness," (b) a capacity to mobilize resources, and (c) a degree of institutionalization and hierarchy.[2] Polities do politics, with politics being the conflicts over who gets what, when, and how that make us who we are. It follows that any polity is held together not only by its institutions but also by the mutual struggles that structure it.

This book is an introduction to IR, and introductions to scientific disciplines may take many forms. It may be a rundown of theoretical approaches and where they come from. This is important stuff: obviously, in order to understand the *problematique* of IR—why we ask these questions and not others, and how we ask them—we must have had previous questions and answers that led our inquiry to the point where exactly these things, and not others, have become problems. In order to suggest new answers to old problems and raise new problems, we need an understanding of how we ended up problematizing the stuff we do. The main problem with that approach is that to theorize in the social sciences (as opposed to in philosophy) is necessarily to theorize about specific social phenomena. If you do not know anything about the kind of social phenomena that we study, then how would an introduction to such theories help you? To give an example, how could you theorize about the outbreak of war if you did not know about a number of such outbreaks?

One way of getting around substance-less theorizing is to introduce IR in terms of its subject matter—to give you a rundown of major wars, major treaties, or major states systems. Historical stuff is indispensable data for IR. If you want to know where you are and where you are going, you will need to know where you are coming from. History, then, is what one generation—in this case, my generation, and, one would hope, to some degree also your generation—finds interesting about previous ones. To introduce IR in terms of its subject matter only, however, would be to introduce not the discipline of IR, but the discipline of international history. International history can tell us much about specific phenomena. However, it cannot perspectivize (draw out what the case looks like as seen from one particular perspective), compare (systematically read against another specific social form) or generalize (systematically draw out the degree of specificity of the case under study compared to the whole set or a smaller set of the universe of cases across time and space to which the case belongs) with much rigor, for it brackets theory (Svedberg 2014).

So, without knowledge of our own discipline's theoretical history, we do not know which questions to ask of the data. But, without knowledge of the history of the subject matter that we study, theorizing becomes spectral. My way around this conundrum is to go neither for the theoretical nor for the historical tack, but to try to combine them by starting with the very language that people who have conducted international relations at different historical junctures have used and that scholars of international relations have partially adopted as their own. Hence the title of the book: *Concepts of International Relations*.

What, then, is a concept? In Medieval Latin, *conceptum* meant a draft or an abstract. This meaning is still with us, as when we speak of conceptual art. What I have in mind here, however, is the meaning that goes back to Cicero's classical Latin, and means something conceived.[3] What we study in the social sciences are social facts, that is, what a certain group of people hold or conceive to be true at a certain point in time. These social facts are concrete things with concrete effects.[4] Consider a concept that we all have lived experience with, namely "human."

How do we conceive of what it is to be human, and, in effect, who is human? One answer would be to point to biology. On the one hand, humans are organic and alive, which makes us different from machines. On the other hand, *homo sapiens* is a species of life, of mammal, of primate, of humanoid, the specificity of which lies in being different from other species. So, we are humans because we are not, say, chimpanzees or neanderthals. Another answer would be our psychological faculties: we are the reasoning species (*sapiens* is Latin for knowing), we are the tool-making species, *homo faber*. We are humans because we are neither primarily artificial intelligences working on logarithms, nor primarily animals working on instinct. These are important answers. They, and the biological and psychological traditions that they flow from, are important to the social sciences and the study of IR in that they lay down certain benchmarks for social variation. Our subject matter, however, is exactly that very social variation within those biological and psychological benchmarks, and not biology and psychology as such. We foreground the social and background the biological and the psychological, and we do so in a very specific way, namely by holding that there is a biological and psychological unity to humankind. This unity is important to us as social scientists, for social scientists compare stuff, and comparison is predicated on some kind of similarity between what is being compared. What guarantees the validity of comparing relations between political units over time and space is the biological and psychological unity of humankind (Neumann 2014).

This is not obvious stuff. Historically, the unity of humankind has been in question. When Europeans arrived on what some of the locals called Turtle Island in the late 15th century, a debate ensued among them about whether the locals were humans. One of the most shocking books on the stuff of IR that I have ever read is Tzvetan Todorov's *The Conquest of America* (1984), which goes into the harrowing details of this encounter. The question of human status comes up again and again in world history, not least in the context of colonization.[5] The starting point of the social sciences—that there is a biological and psychological unity to humankind—is not an uncontested one, and is likely to remain contested in the foreseeable future.

So, that's the point regarding humans. The point regarding the *concept* of the human is another one, namely that it is historically variable and contested. This goes for all concepts. There is yet another point to be made about concepts, though, and that is that they are what philosophers call "essentially contested," which means that there is no one to one relationship between the concept and what the concept refers to. Take "human" again. The concept "human" is what linguists call a signifier, and the phenomenon it signifies, humans, is the signified. Historically, the relationship between the signifier human and the phenomenon human, which that signifier tries to capture, is indeterminable.[6] This means that there is no way of pinning down one meaning of a concept at the expense of all others. We already saw this where "human" is concerned, but let's evoke the cliché example: one man's terrorist is another man's freedom fighter. The key here is that there is nothing outside the general context where the concept is used, what we call discourse, that can be used to pin down once and for all what a concept means.

According to one of the major sources of inspiration for this book, the German conceptual historian Reinhart Koselleck, this is what makes a concept different from a word. A word can mean different things, just like a concept can—a pipe can be a tobacco pipe or an industrial pipe, to "bogart" can be to hold on to a joint or to act like the actor Humphrey Bogart, but, with a word, the context will clarify which meaning is in play. If you see a sign in a metro saying "refuse to be thrown here," you know that it means that rubbish should go into that designated bin, and not that you should put up a fight so that you don't end up being stuffed into the very same bin. With concepts, you never know. What is meant with "I'm a democrat," "I'm a Muslim," "It's an intervention," "This war is an ethnic one"? You cannot know definitely, for there are concepts in play, and concepts are by definition many-splendored things.

A key insight, which is also a key challenge, flows from all this, namely that only that which has no history can be defined, as Friedrich Nietzsche formulated it in the *Genealogy of Morals* ([1887] 2009, 14). If concepts mean different things in different contexts, they cannot be summed up in a universally applicable definition. They can be roughly encircled—that is, we may give rough definitions. Which is exactly what Ferguson and Mansbach did when they defined the polity, and it was an unproblematic thing to do, for what they were after was a catchall term. There is also value in definitions like "power is to make somebody do what she would not otherwise have done," or "warfare is to break down a community's will by use of large-scale force," but such definitions hardly exhaust the phenomena of power or war, respectively. They are a way to start an inquiry, not to end it. In order to even begin to sum up a concept, we have to look at different usages of that concept across time and space. This is indeed the way into the study of IR that I am going to pursue here. I will look at around 30 concepts and discuss where they come from, how they are used, and with which effects. Note that I will privilege (that is to say foreground, concentrate on) *analytical* usage, and particularly analytical usage within the discipline of IR. Analytical usage is usage by people who are studying, talking, and writing about a phenomenon, as distinct from, say, everyday usage. For example, analytical usages of the concept of myth cluster around how myths are stories about why we are here and how we can go on, whereas everyday usage focuses on how myths are not true (as in "it's just a myth"). In a sense, to learn a scientific discipline is to learn an analytical language. Some concepts, such as the state, will demand a lot of historical analysis, since they have a rich and often confusing history that you need to know in outline. Other concepts, such as intervention, demand more attention to clashing usages in contemporary debates.

So much for why and how I will concentrate on concepts. This is the point at which you should ask, which concepts? I will give you a comfortable and a not so comfortable answer. When choosing concepts, I have kept an eye on which phenomena are constitutive of and inherent in the relations between polities. The possibility that conflicts may be settled with nonpeaceful means or the possibility that relations between a plurality of polities become so regular that we have a system are not universal phenomena, but they are nonetheless transhistorical in the sense that they crop up throughout history, and in different places. They pop up in different form, this is true, and we should be careful not to generalize where generalization is not warranted, but we are not exactly surprised when we find this stuff. It's the general stuff that international relations are made of, and so we should discuss it. That's the comfortable part.

What should make every social scientist uncomfortable, however, is that the choice of what is central is not self-evident. When I chose these concepts, I did so because I, and not, say, you, dear reader, thought they were important. If I presented this list, which is in the final analysis arbitrary, as natural, I would naturalize the effects of an arbitrary choice. As it happens, this is exactly how French social scientist Pierre Bourdieu defines symbolic violence. Now, power and symbolic violence are not all bad. They create order, and without some social order, humans cannot go about their business. Since we are engaged in scientific discourse here, however, we are under an imperative to try as best we can to justify choices.

One of the ways of doing that is to come clean regarding one's own social position, what we call one's positionality or situatedness. So here's my score on the basic social stuff: I'm a white male from Norway hailing from an old family of civil servants. All of those factors—ethnicity, gender, nationality, class—have conspired in me choosing the concepts that I have chosen and also how I will be discussing them. So has my so-called secondary socialization, that is, my education: I studied political science and social anthropology in my home country as well as in Britain, and I have worked primarily on the geographical areas of Northern Europe and Russia. So, yes, this book will be Euro-centric, in the sense that I will perpetrate the symbolic violence of privileging European experiences when I talk about international relations (for a counterpoint, see Ringmar 2017). I have taken some measures to alleviate the effects, such as sprinkling the chapters with non-European examples and including a chapter on Euro-centrism and postcolonialism, but you should nonetheless beware that you are in for a variant of what Americans call Western Civilization, where the protagonists are mostly dead white males, and take the measures that you think are appropriate in this regard.

The human predicament is that every statement and every conversation happens within a constraining context. Just as every concept comes with a lot of baggage, baggage that we need to know about if we want to make those concepts our own, so every social setting enables and constrains. Some things are simply taken for granted; they are the background against which everything else happens. This is what we call *doxa* (from the ancient Greek word for received opinion). Saying certain things positions us with the majority or orthodox view, while other things position us with the minority or heterodox view. And then there are the things that the social setting simply makes it impossible to say or do, in the sense that if you say them, you come across as at best nonsensical and at worst mentally disturbed. Say "I was Nefertiti in a previous life" in a Buddhist or Hindu setting, and the worst thing that may happen is that someone says "don't make the same mistake twice, say no to reincarnation." Try the same stunt in a university, and you may count yourself lucky if some fellow student will succeed in changing the topic before you die of shame. What explains this variation is that, although the statement is the same, the discourse within which it is made is different.

As used by social scientists, a discourse is a system for the production of statements. The concept was hatched by French philosopher Michel Foucault in order to get a handle on how it is that so many people in the same place at the same time are saying the same things and have them taken for granted.[7] Discourses, then, are preconditions for what you can say, what truth claims you may make, and be taken seriously. A key point is that discourses change over time. Another is that different discourses coexist, so that you may say something within a religious discourse in one moment (say, "usury is bad"), and then something that is the exact opposite in an economic discourse (say, "dividends are good") later the same day, and still both claims will be taken seriously. So, what is true in one context may not be true in another. Discourse is a way of specifying such contexts as historically specific and often overlapping phenomena.

Discourses produce phenomena. Among these phenomena we find humans, understood as social beings; we exist among other things by dint of how the societies within which we live represent the category of human, as well as the other categories by which we are constituted as human beings (see chapter 19). Discourses do not do this uniformly, for any discourse will enable certain things and disable others. Discourses are, if you like, reality studios that produce human subjects and even whole societies. Where concepts have specific effects, discourses have general effects. One way of thinking about the effects of discourse is in terms of practices. A practice is a socially recognized way of carrying out something that can be done well or badly. Socially recognized means that what is done is understood by at least some other people to be meaningful. Note that this means that practices are culturally specific. It is important that the action in question may be performed well or badly, because this underlines how practices involve training, knowledge, and expertise. This also means that expertise in a specific practice is a source of power, for it places you above all the less capable practitioners of the same practice, so to speak. Singing is a practice. Chewing khat is a practice. So are IR-relevant practices like cleaning your gun or writing a good policy memo.

To sum up, since it is hard to theorize without knowing quite a lot of empirical stuff, and since stuff cannot be analyzed in any depth without application of concepts and theory, this introductory book on International Relations is centered on concepts. Concepts are inherently interesting. Historians of ideas and a number of other scholars make them their key object of study. As social scientists, however, we cannot do that. Our job within the academic division of labor is to understand and explain social discourses and practices. We are interested in concepts because they are concrete and tangible ways of entering social worlds analytically. For us, conceptual analysis is a great starting point, but it is not the endpoint of our inquiry. Please keep that in mind as you digest the chapters to come.

Key Questions

What is the difference between a word and a concept?

What are the arguments against forgetting about all the rhetoric and just getting on with the job of analyzing politics?

Notes

1. Traditionally, the name of the discipline is capitalized, International Relations (IR), whereas its subject matter is not (international relations).

2. We will come back to institutions, but note already now that they are different from organizations. As Alexander Cooley (2005, 13–14) puts it, "[a]lthough both structure human interactions, organizations are formal settings, structures, and bodies in which individuals with a common purpose are grouped. Institutions are the framework of constraints under which individuals within an organization operate. Whereas organizations define the actual structures or 'players' of a social interaction, institutions 'define the way the game is played'."

3. From *concep-*, past participle stem of *concipere*, "to take in."

4. For social scientists, effects are a key thing not only about concepts but also about norms and rules, for another way of saying that these have concrete effects is to say that they are constitutive of social life. As John Searle puts it, they "create the possibility of the very behaviour that they regulate" (Searle 2011, 10).

5. A particularly interesting instance of this is when, in the 16th century, the theologian and jurist Francisco de Vitoria (1991) argues that the Spanish Empire's policy toward Amerindians violates their intrinsic human dignity.

6. But consider the alternatives: if the signified should determine the signifier, which is the majority view, then there must be an inherent tie between them, and that, I think, is not the case. If, on the other hand, the signifier should determine the signified, as hold, for example, psychoanalyst Jacques Lacan and feminist Judith Butler, that would mean that material phenomena count for nothing, because they are infinitely malleable to what concepts can do to them. I do not find that convincing, either.

7. As do all concepts, discourse has a history. In Latin, *discurrere* means running here and there (cf. the expression "being discursive") and in everyday French *discours* simply means speech.

Bibliography

Cooley, Alexander. 2005. *Logics of Hierarchy: The Organization of Empires, States, and Military Occupation*. Ithaca: Cornell University Press.

Ferguson, Yale, and Richard W. Mansbach. 1996. *Polities: Authority, Identities, and Change*. Columbia: University of South Carolina Press.

Neumann, Iver B. 2014. "International Relations as a Social Science." *Millennium* 43 (1): 330–50.

Nietzsche, Friedrich. [1887] 2009. *On the Genealogy of Morals*. Oxford: Oxford University Press.

Ringmar, Erik. 2017. History of International Relations Textbook Project, available at http://irhistory.info, retrieved 20 August 2017.

Searle, John R. 2011. *Making the Social World: The Structure of Human Civilization*. Oxford: Oxford University Press.

Svedberg, Richard. 2014. *The Art of Social Theory*. Princeton: Princeton University Press.

Todorov, Tzvetan. 1984. *The Conquest of America: The Question of the Other*. Norman: University of Oklahoma Press.

Vitoria, Francisco de. 1991. *Political Writings*. Cambridge: Cambridge University Press.

2 ✦ State

KEY MODERN THEORISTS OF THE STATE

Georg Wilhelm Friedrich Hegel	1770–1831
Karl Marx	1818–1883
Emile Durkheim	1858–1917
Max Weber	1864–1920

Understood in its widest possible meaning, the history of the state stretches from the very early stirrings of sedentarization—the coming of agriculture—some 11,000 years ago, and up to the present. Understood somewhat more restrictedly, one may place its beginnings with the regulation of landed property in ancient Greece under Draco (ca. 600 Before the Common Era [BCE]) and until today. Although disciplines like archaeology tend to hold on to such definitions, within the social sciences it is customary to date the emergence of the state in Europe to around the time of the Renaissance. The Italian city-states that blossomed in the 15th century (It. *quattrocento*) are seen as a precursor to a territorialized type of political entity that aimed to homogenize that territory by taxing it, by regulating the use of violence within it, and also, and very importantly for IR, by monopolizing the relations between this state and outside polities.

Note also that, in addition to emerging on the tailcoats of the Italian city-states, the European territorial state must in such a reading be seen to emerge in competition with another kind of polity, empire. If "polity" is a general term for political entities, then "state" is a kind of polity that homogenizes territory on the principle that it has one center, the capital, which ideal-typically dominates the rest of the territory, its hinterland, in equal measure.[1] "Empire," on the other hand, is a kind of polity whose territory may be scattered and that is by definition not homogenous, but heterogeneous, in the sense that its different parts are ruled by different logics, and so in different ways. Typically, the center's dominance is a gradient, so that it is heaviest within the imperial capital, and tapers off as one moves toward the empire's outer boundaries.

In the rest of the chapter, I will substantiate all this chronologically by giving you an outline of the emergence of the phenomenon and of the thinking about it. In order to demonstrate the centrality of the term for social life and for the way we still think about the globe at large, however, I will start in media res, that is, headlong, by introducing the key philosopher of the state and also one of the two key philosophers of the coming of modernity, namely Georg Wilhelm Friedrich Hegel.[2] As you may know, one precursor to the social sciences was speculation on the meaning of history, so-called historiosophy. The greatest work of historiosophy is Hegel's *Philosophy of Right* from 1820 (he also wrote more specifically on world history). The protagonist of Hegel's story about world history is, as you may already have guessed, the state. Let me quote from § 259 (1991, 281):

The Idea of the state:

   (A) has immediate actuality and is the individual state as a self-dependent organism—the Constitution or Constitutional Law;
   (B) passes over into the relation of one state to other states—International Law;
   (C) is the universal Idea as a genus and as an absolute power over individual states—the mind which gives itself its actuality in the process of World-History.[3]

The gist of Hegel's argument lies in the final point. The state delivers us into the future. It is incomparably more important than any individual, for it organizes not only one group of people but also prospectively all of mankind, or, as we would say, humankind, into a species that is fully conscious of its own history and its own potential.

There are a couple of unfortunate side effects of this way of thinking about the state. First, it delivers any despot on a plate the perfect excuse for exterminating people who think and act contrary to what the despot thinks is the very "Meaning of History." For example, in the Soviet Union, any discussion of the state began with Hegel. A second unfortunate side effect of Hegel's way of seeing the matter is the resulting understanding of the rest of the world in Europe's image. If the European state is the epitome of reason, the very currency or standard of civilization, then it follows for Hegel that peoples that have not evolved a state are backward. They fall into two categories. First, peoples that have large-scale political entities, but no European-style state, would be barbarians. To Hegel, Indians and Chinese fell into this category. Second, peoples who do not have large-scale political entities he saw as even more backward, and categorized as savages.

There is a direct line to be drawn from Hegel's theorizing about the state, on the one hand, and the emergence of 19th-century international law, on the other. The scheme of civilized, barbarian, savage, also known as the standard of civilization, grounded international law until well into the 20th century (see chapter 16). One of the key effects of the standard of civilization was that territory inhabited by small-scale groups of human beings was declared *terra nullius*—soil that did not belong to anybody—and, as such, territory that was ripe for imperial European conquest. If you were an Iroquois Native American or a New Guinean highlander, Hegel's thinking about the state, and the use made of it by 19th-century international lawyers, was bad news indeed. It categorized you as a barbarian or a savage, respectively, and furnished you with zero discursive resources to fight that categorization. I believe this may give you a glimpse of the centrality of categorization to social life generally, and to political life specifically. It should also be a reminder of the importance of concepts, such as the concept of the state, to political life, for concepts root categorizations, and categorizations have effects. The hatching of political concepts is itself political, not least because, if these concepts become dominant, they have immediate power effects.

Note that the general 19th-century way of thinking about history as evolving in universal stages is still with us. For example, among evolutionists, the scheme first hatched by Elman Service (1962) that humankind evolves through stages that he refers to as bands, tribes, chiefdoms, and states is still widely used.

Archaic States

From the 1820s onward, bones of something that looked like fable animals started to be dug up in Britain. In China, they had long since emerged at regular intervals, only to be categorized as dragon bones and ground into medicine and aphrodisiacs. It was, of all places, in Denmark that the concept of an ancient history for humankind emerged for the first time with any force, and that, too, happened at the beginning of the 19th century. Armed with the animal bones, which one now started thinking of as those of terrible lizards, *dinosaurs* in Latin, as well as new readings of places like Stonehenge, a new discipline, archaeology, started to theorize the emergence of large-scale political organization.

The conceptual breakthrough came in 1877, when Lewis Henry Morgan published his book *Ancient Society*. Morgan hypothesized that polities evolve from a nomadic to a sedentary form. Recall that by a polity, I mean a group of humans that has a self-conscious identity or "we-ness," a capacity to mobilize resources and a degree of institutionalization and hierarchy. Note that the conceptualization in itself was not new, but simply echoed the one presented by Hegel 50 years before, but that it came in a context where it could be propped up by all sorts of archaeological evidence, and spoke to an already formed audience that was keen to listen to what was being said on the topic:

> Morgan highlighted how all forms of government are reducible to two general plans, using the word plan in its scientific sense. In their bases the two are fundamentally distinct. The first, in the order of time, is founded upon persons, and upon relations purely personal, and may be distinguished as a society (*societas*). The gens is the unit of this organization; giving us the successive stages of integration, in the archaic period, the gens, the phratry, the tribe, and the confederacy of tribes, which constituted a people or nation (*populus*). At a later period a coalescence of tribes in the same area into a nation took the place of a confederacy of tribes occupying independent areas. [. . .] The second is founded upon territory and upon property, and may be distinguished as a state (*civitas*). (from Leacock's preface to Morgan 1963, 6)

This is not the place to review later archaeological conceptualizations of ancient states, but one attempt of particular interest to IR should be mentioned. This is the peer polity interaction model of Cambridge archaeologist Colin Renfrew and colleagues, where the point is to study the emergence of, say, Sumer or Greece as a case of emergent clusters or systems of polities, rather than the emergence of polities on an individual basis. As seen from IR, this sounds like an eminently reasonable idea.

Renfrew observes that "early state modules" tend to cover an area of approximately 1,500 sq. km (Renfrew and Cherry 1986, 2). In many early civilizations their number is on the order of 10, within a factor of two or so. Indeed, early state modules may be seen as the territorial core area of that civilization:

These usually include closely similar political institutions, a common system of weights and measures, the same system of writing (if any), essentially the same structure of religious beliefs (albeit with local variations, such as a special patron deity), the same spoken language, and indeed generally what the archaeologist would call the same "culture," in whatever sense he might choose to use that term. The individual political unit—the states—are often fiercely independent and competitive. Indeed, not uncommonly, one of them may come to achieve political dominance over the others, ultimately uniting the cluster into a single larger unit frequently coterminous in its extent with that of the entire "civilisation." This is a *nation state*, sometimes even an *empire*. (2)

The interaction between peer polities (be they an early state module or a cluster of polities less highly differentiated) changes the polities by dint of

(a) competition (including warfare), and competitive emulation;
(b) symbolic entrainment, and the transmission of innovation;
(c) increased flow in the exchange of goods [. . .] In a region with peer polities which are not highly organised internally, but which show strong interactions both symbolically and materially, we predict transformations in these polities associated with the intensification of production and the further development of hierarchical structures for the exercise of power. (8)

Here we have an outline of what a social science of early complex states needs, namely a framework that is relational and that defers to empirical analysis on the question of which fields of social life have played what role for state building.

Early Theorizing

But let's return to early social science theorizing of the state. Hegel is the ghost in Morgan's book *Ancient Society*, which is an early example of social science theorizing of the state. Furthermore, Hegel and Morgan play straight into one of the key 19th and 20th century conceptual traditions of the state, namely the Marxist one.

Morgan's contrast between a "society" and a "nation" assumes mobile or nomadic groups versus a settled nation. In *The Origin of the Family, Private Property and the State* ([1884] 1972), Karl Marx's key collaborator, Friedrich Engels, latched onto Morgan's reflections on settlement and property, and synthesized them with Marx's analyses of capital accumulation. For Engels and Morgan, the thing to note is that the world was once peopled by nomads, organized in person-based political structures, only to be replaced by settled populations that adopt the state as the principle of political organization. In this sense, the term "state" is reserved for settled populations.[4]

However, Marx and Engels's most famous pronouncement on the nature of the state hails from an earlier and explicitly political work, the 1848 *Communist Manifesto*, where the state is reduced to a material extension of class interest: "The executive of the modern state is nothing but a committee for managing the common affairs of the whole bourgeoisie."[5] It is a good line to pump your fist in the air to, but it flies in the face of Engels's own later work, as well as of Marx's earlier work, where the state is seen as an institution that mediates between class interests in the more general interest of social order. There are insights to be had at both sides of this argument. The state clearly reflects class interests in a lopsided way, but equally clearly, I think, it would be hasty and superficial to reduce the state to a class monopoly, for we have numerous examples of how the state is the primary force behind class compromises, too. One key example concerns the emergence of the welfare state, which was initiated by the conservative German statesman Otto von Bismarck in the 1870s and then taken up first by liberals and then by social democrats, where the key point was that *all* classes should have a stake in the widening of state activities to care for groups and individuals.

If Marx is one founder of modern social sciences, the Frenchman Émile Durkheim is another. Durkheim's thinking about the state is also clearly Hegelian, although Durkheim tries to distance himself from Hegel's historiosophy by referring to it as mystical. He nonetheless clearly and explicitly cherished the idea that humankind is evolving toward a goal: the world state.

Durkheim's point of departure is how rulers extract from and lay down the law for the ruled, but, contrary to Engels, he sees this as an inevitable and obvious process. Every society is, by necessity, despotic at its base. For Durkheim (1992, 82), the state first incorporates itself as a small cadre, organized independently of society: "The State is nothing if it is not an organ distinct from the rest of society. If the State is everywhere, it is nowhere. The State comes into existence by a process of concentration that detaches a certain group of individuals from the collective mass." When the state is young, it has few interfaces with society, but the more it grows, the more those interfaces multiply: the state becomes enmeshed with society. To Durkheim, as a result, the state becomes more and more democratic. As I will attempt to demonstrate below, Durkheim is on the money when it comes to specifying how state formation begins as a business undertaking by some clan or lineage, only to transmute into something more rooted in everyday interaction.

This is not to say that there aren't problems with Durkheim's account. He was too sanguine about the automaticity of democracy, and, as subsequent French thinkers such as Michel Foucault and Pierre Bourdieu made it their business to point out, he was blind to the costs of the process that he described. He viewed the state as organic, as opposed to viewing it as a field of struggle. He was, like Morgan, an evolutionary thinker in the sense that he saw the growth of democracy as a goal. There is nothing wrong with teleology as such. If you drive down a motorway in Greece and it leads nowhere, there will be a sign to warn you that you have to make a turn. That sign reads "Telos." Telos simply means end. Telos may also mean end goal, but it is a common feature of the human condition that goals exist. Aristotle even refers to one of his four types of causality as teleological, and gives the example of building a house. If the goal of the builders is to build a house, then the fact that this thought exists is a cause of the building of the house. Fair enough; if what it takes for A to cause B is (1) that A is different from B, (2) that A happens before B in time, and (3) that B would not have happened if A had not happened first, then teleological causality exists. The problem for us is not necessarily teleology as such, but the level at which it was postulated, namely world history. How could humanity have a common goal that it did not even know about? That would be bad Darwinism. With no skyhook to a god or to history, we may be tempted to let go of Marx and Durkheim's idea of the state as the common evolutionary goal of humanity.

The third founder of academic social sciences, Max Weber, is famous for his thesis from the essay "Politics as a Vocation" ([1919] 1994), where he claimed that monopoly on the use of force is the key factor in state building. A complement to this thesis exists in the work of economic theorist Joseph Schumpeter, where the state is seen as the institution that has a monopoly on claiming taxes. In IR, we find this dualism of focus between the imperative state of strategy and economy reflected in the institutional-ization of security studies and international political economy as two principal subdivisions of our discipline.

What all three principal founders of the social sciences (Marx, Weber, Durkheim) have in common, and this is stuff that we may still build on, is to conceptualize the state as some kind of configuration of three different entities: a spatial one, delineated territory; an institutional one, central government; and a biological one, people. Each of these has its conceptual history. Think of central government, which began as the king and his men on horseback performing raids and taking tribute, continued with institutionalizing middlemen who stood for taxation, and culminated in the emergence of bureaucracy. The last step so far is the emergence of what French philosopher Louis Althusser called the ideological state apparatuses, by which he meant societal institutions such as schools and hospitals that govern through economic incentives and fear of social ridicule rather than fear of violence. We have arrived at the modern state, which is a nation-state and the topic of the next chapter.

Key Questions:

Is the state defined by its claimed monopoly on the use of organized violence (Weber)?

Is the state nothing but an executive committee for the bourgeoisie (the older Marx)?

Is the concept of state so wide as to be useless?

Notes

1. Max Weber introduced the concept of ideal type as a methodological device, that is, as a way to make the specific stuff that he studied relevant to more stuff; to be able to generalize, if you like. The basic idea is that the analyst maximiz-es the inherent rationality of what is studied into an ideal (which is to say, not real) conceptualization of a phenomenon. The ideal type may then be used as a baseline when one studies other variants of the same phenomenon. For example, Weber drew up an ideal type of the bureaucrat (e.g., all written casework and no personal biases) in order to study bureaucrats across time and space. The ideal type (in this case, the ideal bureaucrat) never existed and never will exist, but the postulate is of analytical value, for it helps us to capture what is specific about, say,

bureaucrats and bureaucracy under the second president of Indonesia, General Suharto (1968–98).

2. The other one is Immanuel Kant, who will crop up in chapter 14.

3. You get a gist of Hegel's project, and also of his style, by reading the rest of the paragraph: "The state as actual is essentially an individual state, and beyond that a particular state. Individuality should be distinguished from particularity; it is a moment within the very Idea of the state, whereas particularity belongs to history. States as such are independent of one another, and their relationship can consequently only be an external one, so that there must be a third factor above them to link them together. This third factor is in fact the spirit which gives itself actuality in world history and is the absolute judge of states. Admittedly, several states may form a league and sit in judgement, as it were, on other states, or they may enter into alliances (like the Holy Alliance, for example), but these are always purely relative and limited, like [the ideal of] perpetual peace. The one and only absolute judge which always asserts its authority over the particular is the spirit which has being in and for itself, and which reveals itself as the universal and as the active genus in world history" (Hegel [1820] 1991, 281–82).

4. It is easy to spot Charles Darwin's thinking on evolution here, but even more basically, Morgan and Engels are in synch with the broad sweep of European 19th-century political thinking, be that in an explicitly teleological guise as in Hegel, or in the more implicit version of Kant, himself a sometime geographer and, it could be argued, early anthropologist.

5. Available as https://www.marxists.org/archive/marx/works/1848/communist-manifesto/ch01.htm, retrieved 22 February 2018.

Bibliography

Durkheim, Émile. [1950] 1992. *Professional Ethics and Civic Morals*. London: Routledge.

Engels, Friedrich. [1884] 1972. *The Origin of the Family, Private Property and the State*. London: Penguin.

Hegel, G. W. F. [1820] 1991. *Philosophy of Right*. Cambridge: Cambridge University Press.

Morgan, Lewis H. [1877] 1963. *Ancient Society: Researches in the Lines of Human Progress from Savagery through Barbarism to Civilization*. Preface by Eleanor Burke Leacock. New York: Meridian.

Renfrew, Colin, and John F. Cherry, eds. 1986. *Peer Polity Interaction and Socio-Political Change*. Cambridge: Cambridge University Press.

Service, Elman R. 1962. *Primitive Social Organization: An Evolutionary Perspective*. New York: Random House.

Weber, Max. [1919] 1994. "Politics as a Vocation." In *Political Writings*, edited and translated by Peter Lassman and Ronald Speirs. Cambridge: Cambridge University Press.

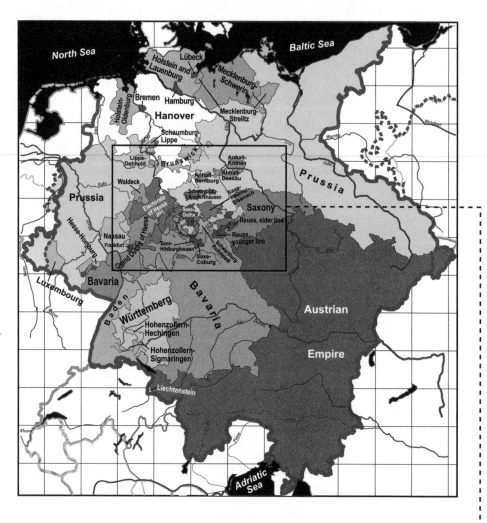

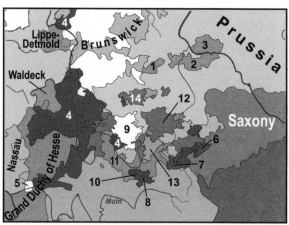

PULLOUT LEGEND

1 – Anhalt-Bernburg
2 – Anhalt-Dessau
3 – Anhalt-Köthen
4 – Electorate of Hesse
5 – Frankfurt
6 – Reuss, elder line
7 – Reuss, younger line
8 – Saxe-Coburg
9 – Saxe-Gotha
10 – Saxe-Hildburghausen
11 – Saxe-Meiningen
12 – Saxe-Weimar-Eisenach
13 – Schwarzburg-Rudolstadt
14 – Schwarzburg-Sondershausen

Map of German small states before German unification. (Courtesy Wikimedia Commons)

3 ✦ Nation-State

In the emergence of the state as discussed in the previous chapter, one change stands out. This is the change from seeing the sovereign being legitimized by God to seeing him legitimized by the people. This change would have been impossible without the changes that the concept of the people underwent, in the name of nationalism. But, in case you should think that religion decamps from the state project when state rule stops being guaranteed by God and starts being guaranteed by the people, consider the welfare state. Michel Foucault suggested that the welfare state, and in some measure the European state generally, does not only have one origin, namely the tradition from the ancient Greeks of the free citizen, but also a dirty, in the sense of suppressed, origin, namely the Christian tradition of the shepherd. The welfare state, Foucault argued, is conceptualized as taking care of us from cradle to grave, just as Christians conceptualize Jesus as the good shepherd who watches over every step of every sheep in his flock.

During the European 18th century, "the people" was conceptualized as the leading class that stood up to the more or less autocratic king. That leading class would traditionally be the aristocracy. From the middle of that century, however, the new middle classes—traders and thinkers, basically—hijacked the concept of the people for their own uses. The most blatant example is of course France, whose 1792 revolution was all about how the middle classes took on the old aristocratic power structure, but we are talking about a European-wide phenomenon here. Note that history repeated itself during the first decades of the 20th century, when the increasingly important labor movements hijacked the concept of "the people" for themselves. State and people form a conceptual pair, in the sense that the people is one of the three elements of the state; specifically, the one that government governs.

There are parts of the world, Germany and Russia, for example, where the concept of the people (*das Volk*, *narod*) is absolutely central to political life. In English parlance, however, the key concept is "nation." The concept has two origins. One is republican and primarily French, with the nation seen as consisting of the citizenry. Another is organic and German, with the people seen as consisting of culturally and ethnically similar individuals. Early theorists like Hans Kuhn were right in stressing this French-German divide, but we should not forget that there were nonetheless organic thinkers in France, and republican or at least liberal thinkers in Germany. The opposition is not an absolute one. The key political outgrowth of the concept of nation is nationalism, the German-inspired political doctrine that people who are culturally similar—often but inaccurately simplified to people who speak the same language—should also share a state (see chapter 8). This is the definition of Ernest Gellner (1983), who stresses how industrialization supplanted people's concrete communitarian village life with a colder and more abstract life in the cities. Some new kind of community was needed to comfort displaced peasants, and one comforter became the nation, a metaphorical, more abstract, and much larger community that took the place of the village as a home. By contrast, Benedict Anderson (1983) stresses the importance of the printing press for this phenomenon. The printing press reduced the importance of the class privilege of knowing Greek and Latin, gave a new importance to the written word (e.g., Protestantism), and homogenized culture accordingly. The third big name of the heyday of nationalism studies in the 1980s and 1990s, Anthony Smith, stressed how the history of nations in Europe was not a fruit of the 19th century, but went back to the late Middle Ages. Nationalism, understood as the idea that it should be politically relevant what language some peasant spoke, however, was strictly a fruit of modernity.

The principle of the nation-state has since spread across the globe and wrought untold damage, by breaking up already existing societies by sometimes introducing and always reinforcing the concept of ethnicity. In China, until a century ago, the Manchu dynasty that had ruled for 300 years was ethnically distinct. Today, only a few thousand Manchu speakers exist. The latest converts to the doctrine of nationalism are to be found in Central Asia where, during the quarter century since the breakup of the Soviet Union in 1991, we now suddenly have fully fledged histories for all the titular nations in the area, and are also blessed with the kind of often state-orchestrated ethnic clashes that characterized the era of the nation-state in Europe as well. State and nation may have started as European concepts, but they are now global.

The reasons are sundry. One is that war made the state, and the state made war, as the late Charles Tilly (1992) of Columbia University put it in *Coercion, Capital and European States*. The state is a good fighting force, for it mobilizes a public, not least so that they can pay taxes, which may in turn be used to build an even stronger army.[1] In a self-help system like the states system, where there is nothing to prevent war, every polity has a strong incentive to copy the institutions of the leading ones (see chapter 7). If the state is the war-fighting force of choice, and war-fighting is necessary to survive in a self-help system, then it follows that turning a polity into a state is a matter of survival for that polity. Put differently, in a system dominated by states, other polities that are less efficient at mustering resources for and waging war will be obliterated. Another reason why the state spread to cover the entire globe was what we may call colonial symbolic entrailment. With European nation-states lording it formally or informally over the entire globe, the state became something to emulate not only for its efficiency but also because this way of ordering a polity was *the* high-status way of ordering a polity.

Transplanted Concepts

When a social phenomenon is transplanted from one context to another, it always changes, for phenomena take their meaning from relations to other phenomena. So, when the concepts for state and nation were transplanted from a European to another regional setting, they changed. It may therefore be misleading to say that the Western social form of the state has been globalized, for although the general form of the European state was definitely an impetus for state formation in the rest of the world, the resulting forms were not themselves Western. The concept of the state arrived only to confront older, overlapping, and competing conceptualizations of what a polity should be. The result was hybridization. Let me give two quick examples, namely the modern African state and the modern Middle Eastern state.[2] Africanist François Bayart, in his book *The State in Africa: The Politics of the Belly* (1993, xvii), makes the key point that the state in Africa is dissimilar from the European state:

The authors of Nigeria's draft constitution in 1976, for example, defined political power as "the opportunity to acquire riches and prestige, to be in a position to hand out benefits in the forms of jobs, contracts, gifts of money etc. to relations and political allies."

Note the affinity between such an understanding of the state and the conceptualization that we found in the *Communist Manifesto*. To complement an analysis that sees the state as imported from abroad, Bayart stresses how

the dominant groups who hold power in black Africa continue to live chiefly off the income they derive from their position as intermediaries vis-à-vis the international system. Revenue from agricultural surpluses seems—with some exceptions of which the Ivory Coast ironically (given its history) is one—to be less great than those derived from levies on mining exports, miscellaneous imports, foreign investment or even development aid. [. . .] Far from being the victims of their very real vulnerability, African governments exploit, occasionally skilfully, the resources of a dependence which is, it cannot ever be sufficiently stressed, astutely fabricated as much as predetermined. (Bayart 1993, 25–26)

Note that, since conceptualizations of political leadership vary globally, the result of the clash between a European-imported understanding of the state and a locally evolved understanding will produce vastly different results. This is as true for the United States as it is for China (where Western models tended to be mediated twice, first via Japan and then via the Soviet Union) and the state in the Middle East. Note also, and here the Middle East is a very good example, that the European colonial experience is just the latest of a long series of colonial experiences that have shaped today's polities. Where the Middle East is concerned, it is also, perhaps even more, important to look at the Ottoman experience than the European one. You will recall that the Ottomans ruled these areas much longer than did European powers, and that their representations of colonials, say Arabs, were remarkably similar to later European representations, particularly after modernity hit Istanbul (both European and Ottoman, and for that matter Persian, representations of Arabs revolved around the alleged backwardness of nomadism).

Ottoman rule in the Middle East was predicated on a standard political technique that will be discussed in more detail in the following chapter, namely the imperial one of using middlemen to rule. The Ottomans would conquer an area militarily and, particularly if it was a far-flung area whose leaders put up stiff resistance, say the Mamluks of Egypt, leave the social and political structure largely intact. The Mamluks, or whoever ruled the area in question, would continue to rule, but, formally, they would be the clients of the Ottoman sultan, who would be their patron.[3] How could clients of the Ottomans get as much leeway to rule their own polity as possible? First and foremost, by playing the Ottomans off against other patrons. As seen from the point of view of the Mamluks, or of any other group of middlemen who were clients to the Ottomans, it was therefore not all bad when other empires started to take an active interest in their polity. It did mean that they could be caught in a squeeze between two vying patrons, yes, but at least it also meant that they could play off a new patron against their old one. Examples would be how the khans of the Crimean khanate played Russians against Ottomans in the late 18th century, or how Muhammad Ali played the French against the Ottomans in Egypt in the first half of the 19th century. With European powers trying to increase their formal control into the entire area during the 19th century, this fight between the Ottomans and some European power over who should be patron became a region-wide phenomenon.

Now, Einar Wigen (2016) has pointed to an important consequence of this history for present-day post-Ottoman states. Their political elites come out of a centuries-long tradition of owing their power to two factors: control of people and territory, and patronage from some superior power. Wigen's hypothesis is that this latter factor, the search for patronage, is alive and well in many post-Ottoman states, and lends a particular flavor not only to the alliance politics of these states but also to wider questions of what kind of states they are. The European state is supposed to be sovereign, which means that it recognizes no power above it (see chapter 17). The argument here is that, due to what a social scientist would call path dependence, which means that things are as they are now because they follow on from a series of previous events, many post-Ottoman states do not seem to think of sovereignty in this way. Relations between, say, Lebanon and France, Syria and Russia, Egypt and Britain, and also the United States, arguably go beyond alliance politics and look rather like patron-client relations. One way of understanding this is as a path-dependent remnant of Ottoman practices. Theoretically, the point is that hybridization is afoot. Just as certain African states specialize in extracting economic resources from external agents, certain post-Ottoman states specialize in extracting patronage, and this does something to how we must understand them as states.

Polities that exist within a common and overarching polity will tend to hybridize more than polities that do not. One upshot of this is that present-day states differ among other things according to previous experiences with being part of an empire. Empire will be the topic of the next chapter.

Key Questions

Does it make analytical sense to consider the concept of state without the concept of nation?

Is the state an exclusively Western phenomenon?

Notes

1. Tilly's entire approach to the study of comparative state building turns on what kind of mix of capital raised by taxation and use of force that goes into any one project: "If urban ruling classes played important parts in the initial consolidation of a given state (as they did in Holland), long afterward the state bore their imprint in the form of bourgeois institutions. If a state originated in conquest of largely rural populations (as did successive Russian empires) it continued to offer little scope to such cities as grew up in its midst; in such regions, large nobilities grew up as monarchs granted fiscal privileges and substantial local jurisdictions to arms-bearing landlords in return for their intermittent military service" (Tilly 1992, 58).

2. Yes, by speaking regionally, I am speaking in headlines, about Africa as about Europe. If one wants to cover the basics, does one have a choice?

3. While the sultan was the formal head of the Ottoman Empire, it was the grand vizir and his office, the Porte, that took care of running business affairs.

Bibliography

Anderson, Benedict. 1983. *Imagined Communities: Reflections on the Origin and Spread of Nationalism*. London: Verso.

Bayart, François. 1993. *The State in Africa: The Politics of the Belly*. London: Longman.

Gellner, Ernest. 1983. *Nations and Nationalism*. Ithaca: Cornell University Press.

Tilly, Charles. 1992. *Coercion, Capital and European States*. Oxford: Basil Blackwell.

4 ◆ Empire

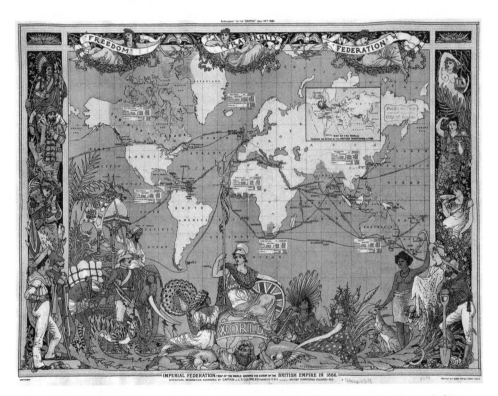

Imperial Federation. Map of the world showing the extent of the British Empire in 1886. The words "Freedom, Fraternity, Federation" on the top banner contrast nicely with the racialized hierarchy depicted at the bottom. (Courtesy Wikimedia Commons and the Norman B. Leventhal Map Center, Boston Public Library [https://www.leventhalmap.org].)

States are often taken to be the most important form of polity in recent history, or even in world history. They have a strong contender, though, and that is empire. Where states are supposed to be sovereign and relatively homogeneous political units, empires are conglomerates of a center and peripheries, where the peripheries are subordinate to the suzerain center and have different kinds of relationships to that center. Suzerainty simply means that there is one power center around which other polities are subordinated. This was the structure of early large-scale polities like the Akkadian Empire, of Eurasian steppe empires like the 13th century Mongol empire, of the 16th and 17th century overseas polities focused on Spain and Portugal, and again of the self-proclaimed European empires of the 19th century. Note the ambiguity of so-called modern European states: they tend to go from having an imperial to having a state structure in Europe, but, concurrently, they tend to be cores of empires in a global context. For example, by the end of the 19th century, France, understood as the hexagonally shaped territory in the European heartland, was a nation-state, but France understood as the global polity centered on Paris and the hexagon was an empire.

Let's start with an analytical definition of empire. Charles Tilly defined empires in two steps. First, empires consist of a center (typically a cosmopolitan metropole) and peripheries (colonies). This is a radical underspecification, though, for polities are by definition hierarchical, and hierarchies have a center. What makes empire a special category of polity is, therefore, their second characteristic, which is that there are different power relations (or "contracts," as Tilly names them) between the center on the one hand and each of the different peripheries on the other. The middlemen who run a certain periphery have a unique relationship to the center. This is what Tilly calls heterogeneous contracting. We are on the level of ideal types here. The reality of, say, the relationship of each *Land* (federal subject) in Germany or each state in the United States to the center is different from that of any other *Land* or state, but ideally these relations are supposed to be the same—the state, even a federal state where laws vary somewhat among its constitutive parts, is supposed to be a homogenous political space. Empires are not.

Let's go back to the first large-scale polities in human history, which emerged some 5,000 years ago. Mesopotamia, Egypt, and the others would have centers, and then they would have peripheries. For example, ancient Egypt would run small polities in Sinai as colonies in order to, among other things, extract food from them, offering protection against other empires and other comers in return. Ancient China and Rome would protect their boundaries in order to keep people in and raiders out. They would use various material techniques, such as throwing up earthworks and building palisades (*limes*), in order to achieve this. Once again, food production had a lot to do with it; these boundaries tended to go up where the good agricultural soil stopped. If, for various reasons, these boundaries did not do the job, one response would be to colonize unruly areas. China did this with the Xiongnu, and Rome did it with a number of areas, such as Gaul and Dacia.

In each of the Roman colonies, there would be a prefect—the most famous of these is arguably the fifth Judaean prefect, Pontius Pilate. Pilate was Rome's man. The main middleman was Herod, who ran the place as a polity subordinate to Rome. The Chinese had and still have a particularly striking terminology for categorizing colonial or barbarian subjects. They could be raw, as in untamed by colonial power understood as civilization, or they could be half-cooked or even cooked, that is, on their way to becoming Chinese. Romans used a similar scheme and rated barbarians as more or less wild. Note that it is always a point of contention whether empires acquire colonies first and foremost as a protective move—the raiding barbarians have to be stopped and the way to do that is to bring them under control—or as an aggressive move; the barbarians have resources that the empire wants. Recently, Nicola di Cosmo wrote a highly acclaimed book, *Ancient China and Its Enemies: The Rise of Nomadic Power in East Asian History* (2002), which revised common knowledge that saw the Chinese as reactive to barbarian pressure, by stressing how sedentary Chinese states such as the Chin were actually themselves the aggressors on a number of occasions. Where the British Empire is concerned, historians John Gallagher and Ronald Robinson (1953) made their names with an essay that stressed how challenges on the ground in the peripheries made that empire into an actively expanding one.

In terms of conceptual history, the original meaning of the Latin term *imperare* was "to command" (e.g., the expression "imperious manner")—as when the famous expression "divide and conquer" is reproduced in Latin (where it seems never to have been used) as *divide et impera*. Byzantium (Eastern Rome) was sometimes called, at times self-referentially, and at times by others, an empire (*basileia*). Byzantium held itself to be God's creation. What distinguished the Roman Empire from that of the Byzantines was less the change of capitals (Rome to Constantinople) than it was first and foremost the creation of a Christian Roman Empire (Geanakoplos 1976, 39). Constantine's bishop, Eusebius (ca. 263–339), was responsible for the key conceptual work:

> According to the Eusebian formulation, the emperor is the viceregent of God, the mimesis or "living icon of Christ" ("*zosa eikon Christou*"), and he rules the *Basileia*, the Christian commonwealth, which is in turn the terrestrial counterpart of God's kingdom in heaven. Since there was only one God, it followed inevitably that there could be only one empire and therefore only one true religion. Hence [. . .] unity of empire entailed—nay demanded—unity of religion. (1976, 39)

This idea, that the empire is heavenly guaranteed by the empire being God's vicar (the Christian version) or shadow (the Ottoman version) on earth, crops up in different forms in China and Latin America as well. In the case of the Byzantine Empire, it followed from the central role played by religion in the conceptualization of the undertaking that the chief requirement for admission to this *basileia* or empire was conversion to Orthodox Christianity. Byzantium also made it a key task to proselytize among its neighbors. The empire maintained relations with sundry neighbors, including Germanic peoples, the Visigoths in Spain, the Franks and the Lombards, the Huns and the Avars, the Slavs and the Arabs. A number of these converted. "It is often said," writes Kazhdan (1990, 20),

> that Byzantine diplomacy had a "universalist" or imperial character which was embodied in the idea of the complete coincidence of the "Roman empire" with the civilized *oikoumene*. The Christian world has been conceived of as a complex hierarchy of states at the top of which stood the emperor surrounded by the family of princes.

At the time of Byzantium's golden age, Charlemagne attempted to construct an empire to succeed Rome, and as part of this undertaking he allowed himself to be crowned *imperator augustus* on Christmas Day in 800. Note the continuity here, not only in the aping of Roman titles and Roman rites, but also in what occasioned the use of the concept of imperator, namely a victory over barbarians. In 800, Charlemagne had just beaten the Avars, one of many mainly Turkic-speaking peoples based on the Eurasian steppe that had decided to raid the settled lands west of the steppe and ended up by settling there themselves. The Avars had arrived in the mid-6th century. The Avars were organized in a khaganate, the political order of choice for the nomads of the steppe empires of inner Asia, and it was this khaganate that was given short shrift by Charlemagne.

Charlemagne's victory over the Avars is not very important for our understanding of empire, but his modus operandi after the victory is, for it was all directed toward establishing a particular effect that we call *translatio imperii*. The basic idea behind this so-called translation of empires is that any ruler who is seen to continue a tradition, rather than to usurp to himself the right to rule, will thereby boost his authority. When Max Weber tried to identify what makes rule legitimate in the eyes of the rulers, one of his examples was tradition (the other two were charisma and law), and *translatio imperii* is an example of how rulers create tradition to come across as more legitimate than they would otherwise have been.

There is another reason to stop and consider the Avars, which is that they themselves were what we call a steppe empire, or marching empire. From around 800 BCE, the Eurasian steppe produced empire after empire: Scythian, Sarmatian, Avar, Seljuk, Mongol, Ottoman. We have already touched on the reason why these empires are rarely studied by social scientists today, which goes back to how Hegel considered sedentarism necessary for a polity to be worth studying (see chapter 2). Note, however, how steppe empires and sedentary polities hybridize—the Il-Khans in Persia, the Yuan dynasty in China, and the Ottomans are particularly famous examples of this. Note also how the Ottoman Empire, which established itself in Constantinople after it had conquered the city from the Byzantines in 1453, were also eager to establish a *translatio imperii*. If one compares the key cultic center of the fallen Byzantine Empire, the Hagia Sophia, to the Blue Mosque that the conquerors built next to it, the similarities are striking, and that is no coincidence. You will find that the need to establish a *translatio imperii* transcends differences of religion and cultural tradition. It is well known how all European empires—and also the Americans with their senates and their capitols—have claimed a *translatio imperii* from Rome, but I think it is particularly interesting that the need to establish continuity of rule transcends and trumps cultural homogeneity and so demonstrates something transnational about political legitimizing structures. Another example of this is how, when the British formalized their rule in India in 1858, *translatio imperii* was claimed from the former suzerain, the Mughals that had come and taken over in 1524.

As should be clear by now, empires are ubiquitous throughout the part of human history for which we have a written record. In the West European Middle Ages, the concept of empire was also, and specifically, a resource that the powers that be would wield against the Catholic Church. Empire stood against *sacerdotium*, the heaven-ordained power of the hierarchy of clergy. These two concepts were so-called fighting concepts, that is, concepts that both tried to lay claim to the same area of social life.[1] In this case, the turf fought over was who should be the key power on earth, that is, what Russians call the power vertical—the emperor and his men (empire) or the pope and his clergy (*sacerdotium*)? From 1254, the empire in question was known as the Holy Roman Empire, and from 1512 as the Holy Roman Empire of the German Nation (*sacrum romanum imperium nationis germanicæ*).[2] The Holy Roman Empire was the polity that the so-called Westphalian states tore themselves away from. It hung on to existence until 1806, when Napoleon, who wanted an empire of his own, abolished it.

The polities that tore themselves away from the Holy Roman Empire, and that we refer to as burgeoning states, did not necessarily think of themselves that way. As they tore themselves away from the Holy Roman Empire and also from the *sacerdotium* of the Catholic Church, they often referred to themselves as empires. As an example, we could take Henry VIII's Act in Restraint of Appeals from 1533, which was primarily directed toward the pope in Rome, but which is also significant in our context. Here it is written:

> Where, by divers sundry old authentic histories and chronicles, it is manifestly declared and expressed that this realm of England is an empire, and so hath been accepted in the world, governed by one supreme head and king having the dignity and royal estate of the imperial crown [. . .] to keep [this realm] from the annoyance as well of the see of Rome as from the authority of other foreign potentates attempting the diminution or violation thereof. (quoted in Armitage 2000, 11)

Here "empire" refers to a political unit that is bound by no foreign power. From the perspective of conceptual history, the point here is that "empire," in the core period of this process (the 16th century and the first half of the 17th century), refers to "sovereign state." When the states system was established, it was the term "state" that became the common name for this phenomenon, whereas "empire" continued to be the designation of the Holy Roman Empire, which continued to exist in the shadows of the states system. We still have a remainder of this meaning of the term "empire" in the juridical description of state sovereignty, where the king is said to be imperator: *rex in regno suo est imperator* ("the king is emperor in his realm").

Parallel to this development, we have the so-called European age of discovery. From the 1340s onward, Portuguese sailors arrived in West Africa. In 1492, Christopher Columbus set out from Europe to India, going west. We still sometimes talk about the "West Indies" when we should be talking about the Caribbean, and we do so because Columbus thought he was about to hit India when he had actually hit what European colonists came to call the "New World" and the Americas. The Spanish Empire that eventually emerged would reach from Latin America to the Philippines. It would sometimes take a letter two years to reach from one part of the empire to another.

In Latin America, there were already large-scale indigenous polities based on agriculture in place—the Inca Empire being the best known—and so Spaniards could proceed to take over by insinuating themselves as the thin new top layer. Spanish Latin America lasted until Spain itself was overrun by Napoleon at the beginning of the 19th century. The same dynamics put an end to direct Portuguese rule in Brazil. Even so, the Spanish and Portuguese Empires hung on to life until the United States put paid to Spanish rule in islands from Cuba to the Philippines in the 1890s, and Portugal finally gave up on Mozambique, Angola, and sundry islands as a result of that rare thing, a democratic military coup, in Lisbon in 1974.

In North America, by contrast, there were no large-scale polities to be conquered. True, north of the so-called Pueblo or village Indians in and around today's New Mexico, there were agricultural villages along the Mississippi, but once Europeans reached there, the indigenous populations had already been wiped out by the diseases that preceded Europeans wherever they went.[3] As a result, where the story of Latin American colonization is basically one of creolization—that is, of hybridization between a thin new layer of rulers and local populations—the North American story on the other hand is basically a story of settler colonization. In addition to creolization and settlement, the history of imperialism in the Americas is also the history of a third element, namely the introduction of subordinated people from other continents. The plantation economies that Europeans introduced in both Latin America and the southeastern corner of North America were labor intensive. The labor came primarily in the form of slaves imported from Africa, but also eventually as indentured labor imported from Asia.

Only now are we getting to what is often called the "age of imperialism"— roughly the 150-year long period from the Napoleonic Wars to decolonization in the 1960s. This is the second period of European imperialism. It is linked to the first period, which was dominated by the Spanish and Portuguese imperial campaigns and by the increasingly intense trade in goods and humans throughout the 18th century. Note that there was hardly a Western European polity that did not join in. Intermittently during the 17th century, even Courland (in present-day Latvia), which was itself not a sovereign state, had a colony in the Caribbean for some time, namely Tobago. Britain and France dominated, but there was also the Netherlands in and around Indonesia, Belgium in the Congo, and Denmark in the Indian Ocean. Denmark sold the remnants of its West Indian crown colony to the United States as late as 1917 (they are now known as the US Virgin Islands). The modern world was ushered in by an age of imperialism.

All this did not happen without opposition. It should be noted that, in a conceptual perspective, the period of Enlightenment was a period of anticolonialism. Enlightenment thinkers like Voltaire came out strongly against empire. They thought the subjects of a particular ruler should have a say in who ruled them, and how. This was a rather new idea. Importantly for our understanding of empire, it changed the meaning of the concept of "colony." Before the Enlightenment, colony meant something like that which had been split off from a mother unit. The colonies of ancient Greece, for example, were new and independent poleis that did not have that much contact with the mother polis, but they honored the memory of where they come from. After the Enlightenment, the meaning of colony changed, and colony came to mean what it still usually means, namely a polity that is formally or informally dependent on and downtrodden by an imperial center. Enlightenment thinking held that people should decide for themselves, and was therefore against empires and colonies.

Enlightenment thinking did not win the day where imperialism was concerned. With the Napoleonic Wars out of the way, industrialization took off in Europe. There was an increase in the demand for cotton and other resources, and the majority of the world's land mass came to be formally colonized. The project was a self-enforcing one: once colonial rule was formalized, it tended to spread, as the securing of raw materials and territory often involved pacifying and incorporating new territory into the empire. There are even examples of expansion with no immediately obvious motive. One illustration of this from the 1860s involves why General

Cherniaev claimed Tashkent for the Russian Empire, although there existed no orders from above and there seemed to be no specific reason to do so.

In the 1840s, the Enlightenment critique of empire returned in a new guise, as the so-called Manchester Liberals, led by Richard Cobden, argued that imperialism was nothing but a huge outdoor relief program for the upper classes. Instead of the imperialism of the aristocracy, Cobden wanted the bourgeoisie to take over. Free trade should be the organizational principle of international relations, so that there would be as little contact between states as possible, and instead as much contact between peoples—read traders—as world infrastructure could possibly hold. In the early 20th century, economist and social philosopher Joseph Schumpeter formulated a full-fledged theory of imperialism along Cobdenite lines. He argued that, in an increasingly bourgeois European world that saw less and less room for the old aristocratic specialty of use of force, the aristocracy had to turn outward to find places where they could apply their comparative advantage, the said use of force. Hence, imperialism should be understood as an atavistic by-product of European economic development.

Schumpeter's take on imperialism was an isolated one. However, the major conceptual development of the late 19th century we find in Germany, where social democrats used "imperialism" to denote the expansion of other European powers. Germany set in train a movement that would eventually make it impossible to use "imperialism" as a positive term used about one's own group. "Imperialist" became a negatively loaded concept used about others. Marxists came to evolve theories about how their Others—the capitalists—engaged in an ever-expanding enterprise that had its roots in economics (either trade or export of capital). The most famous of these Marxist theories is Vladimir Lenin's.

Lenin drew on Marxist and socialist thinkers (another crucial influence was the English liberal John Hobson, who was himself inspired by Cobden) to argue that imperialism was simply the culmination of capitalism. Capitalism, Lenin argued, had to expand to survive. Capitalist states could not cooperate with one another beyond sharing spoils, for what drove capitalist states was capitalist class interest, and capitalists were a national class. When the correlation of forces between different capitalist states changed, the capitalists in the rising state would demand more resources. As long as capitalists had the option to expand globally, this struggle could be solved by the rising state grabbing new land and new labor some place overseas. However, now that capitalism had expanded to envelop the whole world and there was nothing left to carve up, Lenin argued, the result was inevitable: a global war. Lenin published his pamphlet *Imperialism: The Highest Stage of Capitalism* in 1917, as the First World War was raging, and offered his theory of imperialism as an explanation of the Great War (rising Germany could not be accommodated by the other capitalist great powers, so war broke out). What would come after the highest stage of capitalism was of course communism, and under communism, there would be no imperialism, for imperialism was a capitalist phenomenon that would go to its grave together with capitalism. Communist states would be animated by the class interest of workers, and workers were an international class with internationalist class interests. The coming of communism would therefore also mark the end of war.

Lenin was wrong on both these counts.[4] Imperialism antedates capitalism, and it survived communism. The polity that Lenin helped found, the Soviet Union, may also be understood as an empire. The Marxist stress on how empires extract economic resources may also be faulted, for we have examples in world history of empires that did not succeed in extracting from their peripheries more than they had to pay to maintain them. The Soviet Union itself may be such an example—it is not clear that the flow of resources from Eastern Europe to the Soviet Union in the period from 1945 to 1991 exceeded what it cost the Soviet Union to maintain its grip on that region. There were periods when China seems to have paid more in gifts to their nominal subjects that what it got back in tribute.

To sum up, empires are polities where a center rules various peripheries by the use of middlemen and where the relationships between the center and the various middlemen are based on different deals—so-called heterogeneous contracting. One way of thinking about the period from 1800 to 1950 is that the key European polities were hybrid creatures: they were states at their European core, and, by dint of their overseas (or, in the case of Russia, overland) peripheries, empires globally. This is an ideal-typical take, for all empires by definition follow a gradient, where there is direct and strong rule at the core, and gradually more indirect and weaker rule toward the boundaries.

Let me end with a recent attempt to treat formal empire as one of four ideal-typical ways of organizing relations between polities that differ in power resources. David Lake (2009) sees cooperation between states as a matter of relational contracting, akin to how business firms choose their cooperation partners and organize relations with them. He argues that states choose the form of their cooperation with other states after having assessed the expected opportunity and governance costs of all available alternatives against one another. On this basis, he proposes a typology of dyadic relationships between states, reflecting four possible combinations of expected high/low opportunity costs with expected high/low governance costs. First, when the internal power balance between the two parties is fairly equal, and when the expected governance costs of cooperation are considered high, Lake argues that states are likely to opt for alliances. This is the least formalized and least hierarchical alternative of all possible forms of relational contracting. Alliances, in Lake's definition, are relationships between two states that are formally equal in power, and that have chosen to pool their resources for mutual benefit. At the opposite end of Lake's scale, we find formal empires. Here, the power balance between the parties is asymmetrical, and, within the dyad, the stronger power governs the weaker through formal structures and mechanisms. In between alliances and empires on the scale, Lake identifies two additional, intermediate forms of relational contracting. In protectorates, there is a minor power asymmetry between the parties. In informal empires, the more powerful state governs the minor on an informal basis. Lake's rationalist analysis suggests one possible reason why the 19th century was dominated by formal European empires whereas the latter half of the 20th century was dominated by American hegemony.[5] In the former case, European states had overwhelming power resources, and could colonize other polities at fairly low cost. In the latter case, the costs had risen, so as seen from the dominant power, establishing informal hegemony rather than formal empire now proved a more cost-effective way to get stuff done.

Key Questions

In what degree does empire depend on cultural hegemony for its legitimacy?

What characterizes the social form of the empire?

Is empire the default form of human society?

Notes

1. A central source here is Dante's *De Monarchia* from 1312, which sides with the emperor against the Catholic Church from the viewpoint of a group of polities caught in the middle (the Italian city-states).

2. Hitler could call his polity the "Third Reich" by counting the Holy Roman Empire as the first Reich (a concept that goes back to pre-Roman contact kings of Germanic peoples, some of whom were called *reiki*) and the unified Germany that emerged after unifying wars against Denmark (1864), Austria (1866–67), and France (1870–71) and expired in 1918 when Germany lost the Great War (renamed the First World War after 1945) as the second Reich.

3. Europeans, who had been exposed to new bacteria and viruses coming in from the Eurasian continent for millennia, were more resistant to American diseases than vice versa. The only major one that they took back to Europe may, or may not, have been syphilis.

4. But see chapter 15 ("Balance of Power") for a more positive assessment of other aspects of this work.

5. The concept of hegemony is discussed in chapter 19.

Bibliography

Armitage, David. 2000. *The Ideological Origins of the British Empire*. Cambridge: Cambridge University Press.

Cosmo, Nicola di. 2002. *Ancient China and Its Enemies: The Rise of Nomadic Power in East Asian History*. Cambridge: Cambridge University Press.

Gallagher, John, and Ronald Robinson. 1953. "The Imperialism of Free Trade." *Economic History Review* 6 (1): 1–15.

Geanakoplos, D. J. 1976. *Interaction of the "Sibling" Byzantine and Western Cultures in the Middle Ages and Italian Renaissance*. New Haven: Yale University Press.

Kazhdan, A. 1992. "The Notion of Byzantine Diplomacy." In *Byzantine Diplomacy: Papers from the Twenty-Fourth Spring Symposium of Byzantine Studies*, ed. Simon Franklin and Jonathan Shepard, 3–21. Aldershot: Variorum,.

Lake, David A. 2009. *Hierarchy in International Relations*. Ithaca: Cornell University Press.

5 ✦ International, Transnational, and Subnational Organizations

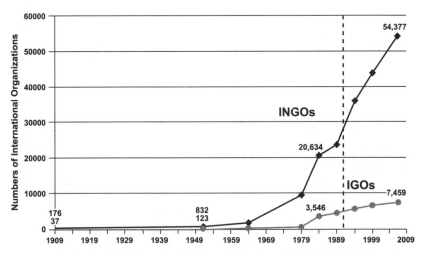

Number of International Governmental Organizations (IGOs) and International Non-Governmental Organizations (INGOs), 1909–2009. (*Source:* "Global Report 2011: Conflict, Governance, and State Fragility," Monty G. Marshall and Bemjamin R. Cole [2011], Center for Systemic Peace, available at https://www.researchgate.net/figure/232621340_fig4_Fig ure-8-Increase-in-the-Numbers-of-International-Governmental-Organizations-IGOs-and)

So far, we have covered two major kinds of polities: states and empires. You will recall that by polity, I meant a group of humans that has a self-conscious identity or "we-ness," a capacity to mobilize resources, and a degree of institutionalization and hierarchy. I also made the point that nations may be seen as a specific category of polities, and that the history of state formation over the last 200 years has also been the history of how states and nations merged into what we call nation-states. Which are the other types of polities that are relevant for us?

The answer is that there are numerous such categories. Let me take but one example: kinship groups. Politics in mediaeval Europe was a game of thrones played by kinship groups. Thus, it is difficult to understand politics in mediaeval Europe without the concept of kinship. In a similar fashion, it is impossible to understand, say, contemporary Chinese politics without realizing that the Long March of the Communist Party spawned party cadres whose sons are now at the heart of the Chinese regime. Kinship is a factor in China, and kinship groups—typically networks congealing around a core of blood relatives headed by a senior male and consisting of adopted members, in-laws (so-called affines), and hangers-on—are definitely polities. If we look at political parties (note, another set of polities) outside China, we find the same thing. US politics is often family-based. Some US Senate seats have been held by four generations of the same family. The Bush and Clinton families were very prominent in American politics for decades. President Trump seems to trust kin more than (other) advisers. The present secretary general of the North Atlantic Treaty Organization, or NATO (another polity), is not only a former prime minister of Norway but also the son of a former foreign minister of the same country. And so on, and so forth. We should not be fooled by the idea that there are traditional societies, where kinship is everything, and then modern societies, where kinship is irrelevant. It is true that kinship is most important in traditional settings, where kinship groups may indeed be the only polity in evidence, but kinship-based polities crops up everywhere (Haugevik and Neumann 2018).

The very terminology we use to talk about other polities than states (and empires) in modernity gives away our state-centric framework: we place them in relation to the state by calling them international, transnational, and subnational actors or organizations. In this case, "nations" simply means states. For example, an international organization (IO) is an organization whose members are primarily or exclusively states.

International Organizations

International organizations, which should really be called interstate organizations, are the simplest to locate. IOs have predecessors in so-called congresses. These were comings together of states, such as the Congress of Westphalia (1648), the Congress of Vienna (1815), and the Congress of Paris (1919), to settle new orders after wars. In the years after the Congress of Vienna, there was even a Congress of Europe. It was in operation formally from 1815 to 1822, when it met annually, and went on informally for decades later. The point here was that Great Powers met to settle stuff that they perceived as threatening to the European order, conferring the expression "working in concert."

Congresses are what sociologists call institutions—patterns of social norms and behaviors—but they are not organizations, for organizations need a formalized and permanent structure. The Congress of Vienna spawned the first example of an international organization. This was the Central Commission for Navigation on the Rhine (1815). It is a typical IO. It still exists, with a membership of five states, a permanent secretariat in Strasbourg, and a staff of a baker's dozen. Perhaps more famous early IOs are the International Telegraph Union (originally Convention, 1865, now a UN agency) and the Universal Postal Union (1874). These early, 19th-century IOs were all so-called functional organizations, which simply means that their raison d'être was to take care of a function or task. This task could be to keep a river open to trade by dredging it of silt and seeing to it that taxation did not overly slow down transactions, or to build infrastructure and maintain the logistics necessary for mail to find its way around the globe.

When the victors of the Great War founded the League of Nations in 1919, it was an important step forward for IOs, for two reasons. First, the League of Nations itself was not a functional organization, but a general one. It was set up to take care of the large and general questions of international relations, not only functional and hence specific ones. Second, the League of Nations served as a spawning site for new functional organizations, such as the International Studies Conference, where people who studied international relations met, coordinated ongoing activities, and initiated new ones. International organizations covering ever more, and more specific, activities came into being.

David Mitrany (1888–1975), a British IR scholar of Hungarian descent, saw the emergence of these functional organizations as a harbinger of a new world order. His functionalist theory of international organizations simply postulated that, as the volume of global tasks or functions grew, and grew rapidly, IOs would take over so many state functions that the state would become obsolete, and we would get a world order based on international organizations. That has not happened, but, since the Second World War, the number of IOs has grown at an astonishing pace and brought a lot of previously erratic and episodic patterns of international interaction into an orderly and more predictable form. The League of Nations did not survive the Second World War, but it had an immediate successor in the United Nations. The United Nations or UN system has continued to expand. It has as its members 193 states and counting, and it has a whole plethora of subsidiary and associated organizations. In addition are all kinds of IOs like, say, the North East Atlantic Fisheries Commission. All told, we are talking about at least 60,000 IOs, probably substantially more.

International Relations scholars have been particularly interested in IO secretariats. How do they work? To what degree are their personnel loyal to the organizations they serve, and in what degree to the states whose passport they hold? Answers vary drastically, and depend on factors like what kind of stuff the IO in question handles, how much pressure different states exert on "their" personnel, and whether the personnel are there for a stint or are looking at a lifelong career in IOs. In a standard introduction to the topic, Ian Hurd focuses particularly on the relationship between states and IOs and argues that there are three principal approaches to this question. One can bracket state members and see IOs as *agents* in their own right. Alternatively, one can see IOs as *fora* within which states interact, or as *resources* on which the state members may draw. As a lawyer, Hurd (2017, 14–15) is particularly interested in questions like which obligations states consent to when they join an IO, to what degree states comply with these obligations, and what the IO can do when states do not comply.

The importance of states to IOs should not be underestimated. Suffice it to say that Norway, one of the states that exert the least direct pressure on citizens working in IOs, nonetheless has two full-time diplomats working on recruitment for the IO slots that open up as a result of Norwegian activity (including monetary contributions) in sundry IOs in and out of the UN system. The personnel question is a way into the key question of in what degree IOs are first and foremost arenas for competing state policies, and in what degree they are better seen as international agents in their own right.

Transnational Organizations

Transnational organizations are harder to define than are IOs. *Trans* means across—Transnistria is a territory that takes its name from being riparian to the Dniestr River, across Dniestr as seen from Moldova, of which it was formerly part. A transsexual is crossing or has crossed from one gender to another. The basic idea is that transnational organizations are agents whose operations cross borders to such an extent that they should be thought of as something more than an extension of the state within which they are based. Such organizations, an alternative name for which is International Nongovernmental Organizations (INGOs), have existed for a long time; the longest-living one is arguably the Catholic Church (the Orthodox churches were nationalized by states). Transnational networks are even older. We have examples of kinship-based networks that must be considered polities as early as the third millennium BCE in Mesopotamia. In mediaeval Europe, they thrived—consider the Hanse or Hanseatic League, the mediaeval German trading organization that was headquartered in Lübeck and had offices from London to Novgorod. The name of the German air carrier, Lufthansa, honors its memory—the name simply means air[borne] Hansa.

Lufthansa is what we call a national air carrier, meaning that it is state owned. The story of most early transnational organizations was that they were taken over by emerging states, but there were exceptions. Again, the Catholic Church comes to mind, but on the list of the 500 or so organizations that emerged in mediaeval Europe and are still with us, there are also names of firms and indeed universities that in a smaller or larger degree have been able to maintain their independence from the states in which they are based.

In the 1970s, the debate about the so-called seven sisters was particularly intense. These were oil companies—five American and two British— that dominated the world's energy trade. These were so-called transnational corporations (TNC), a subgroup of transnational organizations. In what degree should they be considered extensions of the states that harbored their headquarters, and to which extent were they more fruitfully seen as independent agents? Power realists opted for seeing them the former way, while globalists argued for the latter. The issue has become even more intractable since the 1970s. Consider Sony—is it a Japanese firm with an international presence, or an international firm? It understands itself as the latter. Important questions to ask in this regard are where are the HQs, which nationality dominates the leadership, where do taxes go? Transnational organizations are polities, and so inquiry into their characteristics should begin by following the three constitutive aspects of polities— Which we-feeling? What resources? What hierarchy?

Transnational organizations may fruitfully be ordered on a scale from heavily state dependent (e.g., directly controlled state firms) via degrees of independence to independent. Note, however, that the state issue always crops up—given that the Vatican is located within the Italian capital of Rome, it may well be argued that the Catholic Church is dependent on Italy even after its formal independence agreement with Mussolini from 1922. Note also that, in times of war, even the most liberal-minded state does not hesitate to nationalize—that is, make part of the state—seemingly independent firms and organizations that it sees as crucial to the war effort.

A number of transnational organizations prefer to be known as nongovernmental organizations—NGOs. This is particularly so for so-called ideal organizations, which are typically nonprofit, Western organizations set up to champion some cause. Ideal transnational organizations—Amnesty International would be a typical example—tend to start as NGOs in one country and then spread (Hopgood 2006). Amnesty is organized so that it mirrors the state and the states system. Only its headquarters in London can deal with the UN and other IOs. National chapters deal with states within which they are based, and local chapters deal with the local authorities of that state. The social science expression for this is that the state-centric world and Amnesty International are isomorphic, which simply means that they share the same (*iso*) form (*morph*). The fact that transnational organizations institutionalize as replicas of the states system tells us something about the continued importance of state-centricness in IR.

One final point about transnational agency. In their book *Activists beyond Borders*, Margaret Keck and Kathryn Sikkink (1998) trace the existence of what they call transnational activist networks back to origins in the campaign against foot-binding that some Western women initiated in China at the end of the 19th century.[1] Such networks have multiplied. Once again, the key debate surrounding them is to which degree they can be particularly effective before states join the course to end certain practices that are rampant in other states. That happens by dint of various practices, and also by so-called shaming of the state in question. The campaign against female circumcision, particularly the comprehensive practice known as Pharaonic circumcision, is a case in point.

Most nongovernmental organizations or NGOs are based inside a state, though, and they are of course called nongovernmental because they are supposed to be independent of the state. Once again, what "independent" means in this regard is not at all obvious. If you recall Durkheim's understanding of the state from chapter 2, the key point was that the state becomes more and more imbricated with society. So, a Durkheimian would see the state's penetration of society as a positive thing. In light of this, how can NGOs exist at all? And, in a globalized world, how does it make sense to think of an NGOs as being independent not only of the state in which it is based but also of other states? I think the answer to this question is rather straightforward. It is the state that decides what is independent of it, and not society (Mitchell 1992). Put differently, it is the state, and not society, that has the prerogative of drawing the line between the two. It follows that so-called NGOs are dependent on the state by their very nature, for a state can at any time (albeit often at considerable cost) obliterate previously nonstate space and make it subject to state rule.

Consider a blatant example, namely how Russia did away with the entire idea of Russian NGOs some years ago. A law was passed that said that all NGOs had to register, and those that received money from abroad would be branded as foreign agents. In a stroke, the institutionalized part of Russian civil society had become thoroughly policed by the state, for most Russian NGOs had emerged as transnational outfits, and the remaining ones struggled to find nonstate funding within Russia. Western states are historically much more reticent in policing NGOs, but that does not mean that the option does not exist. It does. For good reasons, literature on NGOs circles around the question of how independent they are—perhaps they are not simply nongovernmental, but quasi governmental (QUAN-GOs) or even run as a front by the government and so may be called governmental NGOs (GONGOs)? Indeed, the Russian tradition is to celebrate GONGOs; recall how the tsarist secret police routinely infiltrated social organizations and how Lenin wrote that all social organizations should be thought of as conveyor belts for the state-bearing Communist Party. Note the difference between Durkheim and Lenin, though: to Durkheim, a state is strong if it can get stuff done by consensus and indirectly, without much coercion. To Lenin, the nature of politics is domination and command—who dominates whom (Rus. *kto kogo*).

If nongovernmental organizations are characterized by their claim to being more or less independent of states, then the other kind of subnational organization are parts of states. This would typically mean territorially defined agents such as cities, municipalities, counties, and regions, or functionally defined agents such as tourism boards, export councils, and sovereign wealth funds. In the 1970s and into the 1980s, IR debates were dominated by questions such as whether the state is a unitary actor (a view held by so-called realists), or whether the state is better understood as a bundle of always tussling governmental agencies (a view held by liberals). This was the question of choice where foreign policy was concerned. A central and typical contribution to this debate was Graham Allison's 1971 book *Essence of Decision*, where he analyzed one foreign policy sequence, namely the US response to the Cuban Missile Crisis, as either a question of unitary foreign policy or a question of so-called bureaucratic politics, that is, government ministry and agency tussling, where the President's office, the State Department, the Pentagon, the Air Force, and so forth, all tried to present the crisis from their own perspective and prescribe measures out of their own toolboxes.

Where Allison focused on the foreign policy of one state, Robert Keohane and Joseph Nye looked at the possible repercussions of shifts toward bureaucratic policy for the international system. More specifically, they looked at how relations between certain English-speaking, Western states were more and more dominated by interaction between specific ministries and agencies rather than between governments as such. The research agenda involved generalizing these findings, to see to what degree the world was becoming what they called transgovernmental. Keohane and Nye (1974, 43), defined transgovernmental relations as "sets of direct interactions among sub-units of different governments that are not controlled or closely guided by the policies of the cabinets or chief executives of those governments."

The debate between what came to be known as liberals or neoinstitutionalists, which thought about the increasing way in which the subject matter of IR is institutionalized, and realists, who tended to see all this as a largely irrelevant context for state power politics, turned not only on the importance of transgovernmentalism. The aforementioned questions of the degree to which IOs are arenas or agents, and of the degree in which transnational organizations are extensions of the state where they are headquartered, were also hotly disputed. At some point in the early 1990s, the debate had run its course. The distance between the camps had diminished, so that what was left to quarrel about was not particularly interesting. What was left was basically ritual, as when realists compared the networks of interdependence between states that liberal institutionalists saw as dampeners on states' proclivity to go to war as so much cobweb across the mouth of a cannon. The consensus, and the consensus about agreeing to disagree, was referred to as the neo-neo synthesis, since the state-centric thesis of the neorealists stood against the transgovernmental antithesis of the neoliberals. With hindsight, the entire debate looks like a dry run for the globalization debate that was about to break out, and that is still with us (see chapter 9).

To sum up, international organizations, transnational organizations, nongovernmental organizations, and subnational organizations are important in international relations, but whether they should be conceptualized primarily as extensions of states or as agents in their own right remains a hotly debated question. Conceptually, they all remain derivative of the state by dint of their names, which define them in relation to "nations" understood as states.

Key Questions

Do states work on NGOs or through NGOs?

From where do international, transnational, and subnational organizations obtain their power?

Note

1. Foot-binding involves bending the toes up and back and eventually breaking them, so that the entire foot ends up as a small lump. The practice was heavily favored by the upper echelons of the local patriarchy, as a marker of leisure and also ostensibly for sexual purposes (note that the practice pushed women up on their toes, as do high-heeled shoes).

Bibliography

Allison, Graham T. 1971. *Essence of Decision: Explaining the Cuban Missile Crisis.* New York: Little, Brown.

Haugevik, Kristin M., and Iver B. Neumann, eds. 2018. *Kinship in International Relations.* London: Routledge.

Hopgood, Stephen. 2006. *Keepers of the Flame: Understanding Amnesty International.* Ithaca: Cornell University Press.

Hurd, Ian. 2017. *International Organizations: Politics, Law, Practice, Third ed.* Cambridge: Cambridge University Press.

Keck, Margaret E., and Kathryn Sikkink. 1998. *Activists beyond Borders: Advocacy Networks in International Politics.* Ithaca: Cornell University Press.

Keohane, Robert, and Joseph Nye. 1974. "Transgovernmental Relations and International Organizations." *World Politics* 27 (1): 39–62.

Mitchell, Timothy. [1988] 1992. *Colonising Egypt. With a New Preface.* Berkeley: University of California Press.

REX   LUDOVICUS   LUDOVICUS REX

"Rex, Ludovicus, Rex Ludovicus (King, Louis, King Louis)." English caricature by William Make-peace Thackeray (1811–63) satirizing King Louis XIV of France (1638–1715) and Hyacinthe Rigaud's famous portrait of him (1701). (Courtesy Wikimedia Commons)

6 ✦ Foreign Policy

This chapter tracks the emergence of what we now call foreign policy, goes on to say something about the agents and also the process of foreign policy decision making, and ends by stressing the importance of understanding the place of actor-based approaches to IR for the discipline as a whole.

A policy is a plan drawn up by a representative of a polity to reach a goal. Given that humans are goal-reaching animals, we must assume that policy in its broadest sense is as old as polities. As it is used in IR, foreign policy is a policy drawn up by states for how to coordinate state policy so as to interact with other state and nonstate agents in order to reach certain goals. However, as previously discussed, early state formations were rather undifferentiated. So were the states that emerged out of the chiefdoms of Europe toward the end of the first millennium of our era. The state apparatus consisted of the men who rode with the king (his retinue), and then, when the king settled down, of his court. It is only with the differentiation of the king's offices in the late Middle Ages that we get divisions that are not made according to what is inside or outside of the state, but rather along functional lines. Our first conceptual challenge, then, is to ask when foreign policy became something distinct from general policy.

The first answer to this question offered by the literature is a philosophical one. In *Inside\Outside*, R. B. J. Walker discusses how, in Europe, in the period from the 15th to the 17th centuries, there emerged what we may call an ontic division of the world (with ontic meaning what the world consists of).[1] On the one hand, there was the state, which was incessantly thought of as an ordered realm, subject to lawmaking that could be implemented. The order imposed in the state made it possible for each to progress—inside the state there could be movement toward something better. On the other hand, outside the state, there was no order, only anarchy. In this realm, no progress was possible, only repetition. This division of a world, where the insides of states were seen as ordered and progressive, and the space as it were between states was seen as anarchical, consequently calls for a division of policy into two. Thus, on the one hand, there is policy for how to reach goals within the ordered realm. This is domestic policy. On the other, there is policy for how to reach goals outside the domestic realm. This is foreign policy. There is a sense in which we, as students of state relations, reproduce this distinction between the inside and the outside by dividing our discipline in two: First, there is IR as the study of the states system and other systems of global politics, that is, the outside; and second, the study of foreign policy, that is, the inside.

If we turn from ontology to institutions and ask how the decision-making process of states was actually set up, however, we will not find this division between domestic and foreign until centuries later. An early and numerically very small beginning is to be found in the emergence of diplomatic services, that is, a very small number of people who served the state as permanent ambassadors to other states. This began among the so-called city-states of the Italian *quattrocento* (1400s), and spread to encompass all of Europe in the 16th century (see chapter 13).

Later, and as a separate development, foreign ministries emerged. Cardinal Richelieu is often credited as being the great centralizer of the state apparatus, and rightly so. From 1624 onward, he was the French king's first minister, and he certainly professionalized the bureaucracy of the French state. He did not, however, parcel out the foreign as a separate administrative realm, as should be clear already from the fact that he himself was not foreign minister, but first minister—not in charge of something like a specifically foreign policy, but in charge of policy as such.

Although Richelieu gathered people to look at things foreign around him already in 1624, this early French foray into institutionalizing what was to become known as foreign policy was an isolated one. It was only in the late 18th century that Europe got its first foreign ministries (MFAs; Neumann 2007). During the 19th century, they spread to other sovereign polities around the globe: Russia, Turkey, Siam. Institutionally, then, "foreign policy" is only some two centuries old.

So, one answer to the question of how foreign policy emerged is to argue that, with the emergence of the Westphalian state, the world was divided in two, an inside and an outside. As the political institutions grew in complexity, the foreign was eventually institutionalized as a separate realm.

One central question remains, however: Why did the foreign separate as a specific realm exactly when it did? Halvard Leira (2018) has suggested that this was a result of the emergence of a so-called public sphere—that is, networks of people who eventually made up a somewhat self-sustained entity that we may think of as society. This happened in the 18th century, with liberal England and also France being the key foci. As part and parcel of the emergence of the public sphere, there were journals, magazines, and eventually newspapers. These discussed all phenomena of interest. For the king, it was bad enough to be subjected to criticism for what he himself had done, but it was even worse when newspapers criticized his fellow monarchs, for those fellow monarchs would hold it against him that he let his subjects criticize them. It was as a response to this situation, Leira argues, that the divide between foreign and domestic took shape in English and French political debates. The foreign was simply that which newspapers could not write freely about, that realm of politics that was heavily censored. By contrast, the domestic was an easier (but by no means an open season) target of public debate.

If we combine these three stories, the ontic divide between the inside and the outside of the state that emerged from the late 15th century onward became reinforced during the 18th century by a specific state's policy to curb public debates about "the foreign," and "the foreign" became a separate institutional sphere of the state from the late 18th century onward. You will recall that only that which has no history can be defined. Of course it was the case that Assyrian emperors, mediaeval caliphs, and Renaissance kings had relations with other crowned heads. If we define foreign policy as a policy drawn up by states for how to interact with other state and nonstate agents in order to reach goals, however, then foreign policy as we know it today is but a couple of centuries old, for (a) it must be drawn up by states in (b) roughly the same institutional way that we do it today and (c) the policy must work in an institutional environment heavy with the kinds of nonstate agents that we discussed in the last chapter. I should like to add a fourth factor (d), which is that foreign policy as we know it takes for granted that we think about planning as a rational and elaborated activity. For example, up until the 1840s, the Ottoman Empire did not spend much time either on thinking about war strategy or on thinking about reaching long-term goals, for the granting of such goals was held to be in the hands of God. Given this fact, I question the degree to which we can talk about a pre-1840s Ottoman foreign policy.

Decision Making

If foreign policy by definition involves elaborate decision making, a next question to ask is how this decision making happens. We have encountered two answers to this already. First, there is a person, a head of state or somebody else, who formally defines foreign policy. Second, a key institution is that part of the state that we know as the foreign ministry.

During the 20th century, foreign ministries typically evolved a number of new departments: for trade, for media contact, for security policy, for multilateral institutions, for planning. Such departments are called functional, because they are there to take care of a function or task. There is also another kind of department, namely the geographical one—say, a Latin America Department. Ministries of foreign affairs are forever trying to find a balance between organizing along functional and geographical lines. This is one of the reasons why they are forever reorganizing.

Once the number of departments reaches a dozen or so, it becomes too hard for the leadership of any organization to keep tabs on them. The solution is to put a stop to differentiation into ever new departments, and instead go for differentiation *within* each department. That is done by establishing new sections. For example, a Department of Humanitarian Policy may have sections relating to peace and reconciliation, coordination of development aid, and disaster relief. If the number of people working on disaster relief grows too large, that section may be split into two new sections, on human-made and natural disasters. The key thing is that MFAs have contact points with a number of other domestic and foreign agents, and are supposed to—I repeat, are *supposed* to—serve as the focal point for the decision-making process.[2] To do this, MFAs evolve different institutional units to communicate with other agents inside and outside the state. Here we have another reason why MFAs are forever reorganizing: they need to be as similar as possible to other MFAs so that they can talk to their counterparts, but they also need to communicate with other ministries and agents within the same state. Finding this balance is a challenge that will never go away.

What are these other agents that take part in foreign policy decision making? We have met them already. Domestically, they are other ministries and state organs, as well as NGOs. Some of the decision making will follow functional lines, in the sense that the Ministry for Transport will actually be expected to and often even asked to give input on technical logistical aspects, the Ministry of Defence on security aspects, humanitarian NGOs on humanitarian aspects, and so forth.

Two aspects that are always at least potentially present in foreign policy decision making would be the military and the economic ones. Where the military aspect is concerned, Samuel Finer (1988) suggested in a minor classic on military-civilian relations that the question to ask first is why the military is not *always* in control of foreign policy action. The answer has to do with the degree in which the society in question has different spheres for different social activities. In a society where there are few separate spheres, military might is easily convertible into other kinds of power and so very useful indeed. Modernity is about separating spheres—religious, economic, cultural, military, political, and so on. The further this tendency proceeds, the better the chances are that politics and foreign policy decision making is a separate field that is not just a function of other spheres (military, economic), but is best understood as a master sphere that may draw on all these other spheres when necessary.

If these are broad, general points, note also peculiarities from country to country. In certain states, as a conservative measure, the foreign policy decision-making process is made deliberately cumbersome. One example of this is the American checks-and-balances system, where the president, the Senate, and the judicial system all have key parts to play. If the Senate succeeds in passing a law that, say, bans the export of this or that to state X, then the judicial system will try to uphold that, and to the degree to which the president sticks to it, his hands are tied. There are, of course, ways around this, such as embarking on a route that may lead to war (which constitutionally would need Senate approval) by calling it a police action. This was the course that landed the United States in its war against North Vietnam (late 1950s–1975), which had the effect of splitting the American nation for decades.

In a globalized world, foreign policy decision making will not be a purely domestic affair (if it ever was). In a famous article, Robert Putnam (1988) talks about foreign-policy making as a two-level game; as seen from the key decision maker(s), there are deals to be done with domestic agents, but also with others. For example, the buying of aircraft is a major foreign policy decision, for billions of euros or dollars will change hands, buyback and maintenance deals will tie the buyer state and the state(s) where the seller is located closer together, perhaps over a period as long as half a century, and weapons compatibility will solidify the relationship with certain other states to the detriment of others. Typically, then, the producer and seller of the aircraft will be a national champion, and the state whose national champion it is will be very active in trying to have other states buy from "its" weapons producer. All states do this, but, with the exception of France, Western states typically try to hide the practice. Two-level games are nothing new; only the term is. For example, in Finnish foreign policy decision making, there is an expression, "to tread Peterburgian paths," which means that a Finnish foreign policy agent uses a relationship to Russia or a Russian agent as a resource in domestic Finnish decision making. St. Petersburg was the Russian capital for two centuries, from 1712 to 1918, so the expression does not only bear out the role of foreign agents in foreign policy decision making but also that the phenomenon, which is still on ample display, goes back in time. Imperial, because Finland was a Grand Duchy under Russia from 1809 to 1917. The Petersburgian path is thus an excellent example of path dependence. Note the parallel to the middleman point made in the previous chapter; the overarching logic of present-day international relations may be sovereignty, but that does not mean that there are not other logics, for example an imperial one, afoot as well.

Nowhere is the two-level game logic clearer than in so-called multilateral diplomacy within international organizations. "Multilateral" used to mean that more than one party was involved, but changed meaning after World War II and has come to mean settings where no state agent that wants to participate can be excluded. The UN is a key example; others include the World Bank and the International Monetary Fund. In this setting, international civil servants working for the IOs, diplomats from sundry states, and visiting politicians rub shoulders on a daily basis. The result is a dense social environment where foreign policy compromises and stalemates emerge in an endless series. Linkage—tying one process to another—is common, and the whole thing is an iterative game, where favors and obstructions on one case are not forgotten, but spill directly over into succeeding decision-making processes, the substance of which may be very different.

Most foreign policy decision making is quotidian—it is routine and proceeds at a meandering pace, complete with turf battles and reruns of decisions. Then there is crisis decision making, where the intensity increases, stakes rise, and decision making typically involves the putting out of fires (that is, short-term measures that may not be optimal in the long run but which must be undertaken as a matter of expediency). The most-studied crisis is probably the Cuban Missile Crisis of 1962, when the Soviet Union installed ramps on the territory of its ally Cuba that could dispatch nuclear missiles to the US mainland. The United States answered by imposing an embargo, that is, by physically denying Soviet ships access to Cuba. There was a stalemate, and the Soviet ships turned tail. Such direct, high-risk engagement has come to be known as brinkmanship. The classic on the crisis is the book by Graham Allison that I have already mentioned, *Essence of Decision* (1971). It presented three different "cuts" or models with which to analyze foreign policy: one focusing on the statesman and the international, one on bureaucratic in-fighting between different organs of the state, and one on individual bureaucrats (the latter two are often merged).

Allison's work is a typical example of the IR subfield known as foreign policy analysis, which is devoted to understanding the institutional setup, actual process, and, most particularly, the outcomes of decision-making processes. One of the reasons why Allison's contribution remains a classic is that he has stuff to say about all three temporal phases of the process. Mention should also be made of how identity studies have been applied to foreign policy analysis. "Identity" (from Lat. *idem*, the same) is yet another important concept, for it pertains to how the we-feeling that is constitutive of polities comes into being and is maintained, and with what effects. The traditional way to analyze this is to look for common traits. In ancient times, following common rites and the postulation of common origins were central. With the coming of modernity and nationalism, cultural traits such as language became central (see chapters 3 and 8). In 1969, Norwegian anthropologist Fredrik Barth published an edited book that went on to change how most social scientists think of identity. His key point was that the need to differentiate the "we," or self, from Others was most acute along boundaries. It follows that a polity's we-feeling is not only the result of some old constitutive act and of what we have in common. The we-feeling must be constantly upheld by the social work of maintaining the we in relation to its Others. This is why a Self also has what is called a "constitutive outside," that is, it is perpetually constituted by what the we at any one time holds to be not we, but foreign and Other.

Scholars like Richard Ashley (1987) and David Campbell (1992) took this insight, which was also central to French philosophical thinking in the 1960s, and focused on how foreign policy is an identity-confirming practice.[3] The basic point here is that a Self, for example a state, constitutes itself in relation to its Others; the Self emerges as a differentiation between what is inside and what is outside. This is what it means to talk about Others as a constitutive outside. In this perspective, foreign policy is first and foremost a way to confirm who we are, and only secondly a set of policies geared toward certain specific goals. You will see that this is a critique of how we traditionally think of foreign policy analysis, for what we have here is a different definition of foreign policy than the one centering on goals.

A variant of this project is the one spearheaded by Danish IR scholar Ole Wæver (2002). Here the point is to focus on how the Self that makes up the foreign policy tends to think of and represent polities in its environment as varieties of its own polity. For example, German European Union policy takes for granted that the EU should ideally become a Germany writ large: Germany has a strong central bank, so the EU should have a strong central bank, and so on. The Germany we know today is the result of three wars fought in the 1860s. Before that, there were a number of German polities. What held them together was a political program, romantic nationalism, which dictated that people who shared a culture, with language being a key component, should also share a state (see chapter 3). And so, the German Constitution actually lays down that a state exists among other things by dint of having a state-bearing nation (*Staatenvolk*). Now, when the German Constitutional Court had an opportunity to rule on whether the EU could ever become a state, it ruled against it, giving as its reason that the EU did not have a state-bearing nation (it has, instead, several). Such a ruling makes sense to a German, for this was the way the German state emerged, but it does not make sense to a number of people from other states, say French or Americans, whose states emerged in different ways. Wæver's key point is that the struggle over how to build the EU may be studied as clashing state identity projects in the form of foreign policies that try to build Europe in the image of nation-states.

By way of rounding off this chapter, I should like to repeat that foreign policy is an important part of IR, and that it is crucially important not to mix up what emanates from a study of the specific units of the system (an actor-based approach) with what emanates from the study of the system, understood as a precondition for what units do (IR in the narrow sense). To quote from *The Communist Manifesto* again, man makes his own history, but not under conditions he himself has chosen. There are stories to tell about the preconditions for foreign policy action. There are also stories to tell about the actions themselves, as well as the effects they have on preconditions for further actions. IR as a discipline depends on us understanding the difference and also the interplay between preconditions and actions.

Key Questions

Is foreign policy driven by national interest or identity?

Do foreign ministries remain central to state decision making?

Notes

1. "Ontic" means with reference to being, while "ontological" means the study of that which has reference to being, knowledge of what is. It is a widespread mistake not to keep these two usages apart.

2. If we think systemically about international relations, we note the isomorphism of foreign ministries, how they try to be as similar as possible. MFAs compare notes when they meet and so intentionally stay similar. They also appoint opposite numbers between themselves.

3. These are so-called poststructural analyses. Structuralism approaches social life as a language. The basic idea is that language and society are both relational phenomena, where the meaning of a certain phenomenon resides not within that phenomenon itself, but in its relations to other phenomena. Whereas structuralism tends to focus on static binary oppositions (see, for example, the discussion of structural realism in chapter 7), poststructuralism (with "post" simply meaning what comes after) focuses on the practices that produce phenomena. Categories blend into one another and produce hybridized outcomes. In this perspective, states take their identity from being different from other states, and foreign policy becomes a set of never quite successful boundary-producing practices.

Bibliography

Allison, Graham T. 1971. *Essence of Decision: Explaining the Cuban Missile Crisis.* New York: Little, Brown.

Ashley, Richard. 1987. "Foreign Policy and Political Performance." *International Studies Notes* 13 (2): 51–54.

Campbell, David. 1992. *Writing Security: US Foreign Policy and the Politics of Identity.* Minneapolis: University of Minnesota Press.

Finer, Samuel E. 1988. *The Man on Horseback: The Role of the Military in Politics.* Boulder, CO: Westview.

Leira, Halvard. 2018. "How Old Is Foreign Policy?" Unpublished manuscript, Norwegian Institute of International Affairs.

Neumann, Iver B. 2007. "When Did Norway and Denmark Get Distinctively Foreign Policies?" *Cooperation and Conflict* 42 (1): 53–72.

Putnam, Robert. 1988. "Diplomacy and Domestic Politics: The Logic of Two-Level Games." *International Organization* 42 (3): 427–60.

Walker, R. B. J. 1993. *Inside/Outside: International Relations and Political Theory.* Cambridge: Cambridge University Press.

Wæver, Ole. 2002. "Identities, Community, and Foreign Policy: Discourse Theory and Foreign Policy Analysis." In *European Integration and National Identity: The Challenge of the Nordic States*, ed. Lene Hansen and Ole Wæver, 20–49. London: Routledge.

7 ✦ The States System

WORLD-HISTORICAL LIST OF SYSTEMS OF INDEPENDENT POLITIES

Name	Units	When	Where
Amarna	Early states	17th–13th centuries BCE	Eastern Mediterranean
Ancient Greece	Poleis	8th–4th centuries BCE	Northeastern Mediterranean
Italy	City-states	14th–16th centuries AD	Italian Peninsula
Iroquois	Tribes	14th–18th centuries AD	Turtle Island

When we look at the world from an agent's perspective, that is, from say inside a state and out, we use a foreign policy perspective. In this chapter, we are going to discuss how we may look at the world from outside and in. The key concept for doing this is the states system.

A system consists of units, in this case states, and the relationship between them. A system can be either simple or complex, according to how dense the networks of relations are, and also in terms of how formalized those relations are. When relations are formalized, we say that we have an institution. In everyday parlance, institution usually means an organization. When we use institution as an analytical concept in the social sciences, however, we usually mean a regular (institutionalized) set of practices (as in the legal institution of arbitration or the institution of giving gifts on birthdays) or a social phenomenon that stabilizes such practices (as in "you and your gunshop are an institution in this town, Ruth"). We may draw on this meaning of institution to say that today's states system consists not only of states and relations between them but also of institutions such as war, trade, and so on.[1]

System is a concept that describes the sum total of units and relations between them. It must therefore be distinguished from structure, which is concerned with the *properties of* these relations. Structure is a concept that we use in order to pinpoint and explain a specific logic of a system, something that makes the system more than the sum of its parts (Albert, Cederman, and Wendt 2010). For example, if we think that a certain system is set up so that certain units have better life chances than others, we have identified a particular logic. In order to highlight that this logic is in-built in the system, we may refer to it as structural. If we think that what results from this structural logic is comparable to what happens when agents use physical force against one another, we may refer to the logic in question as structural violence. One way of thinking about a structure is in terms of a wind: you cannot see a wind, but you can infer that it is there through its effects. If you are blue-water sailing, and you do not think about where you are going, it will be easier to sail with a tailwind. By the same token, if you want to do something against the grain, as the saying goes, it will take more work—you are, as it were, sailing against the wind, and that takes more effort. So, other things being equal (Lat. *ceteris paribus*), humans tend to blow with the wind, or, if you like, do the obvious and easy rather than the innovative and hard. In the same manner, if one should guess which newly born baby would have the better life chances, the one born in Togo or the one born in Australia, the guess would probably be Australia. The reason is that there is some logic in the system, unobservable but knowable through its effects that "blow" more wind in the sails of the Australian baby's "boat," so to speak. We will leave the concept of structure now and refer to the concept of system, but I want you to keep in mind that lots of the interesting stuff about a system may be captured in terms not only of agent-centric analysis, that is, what agents do, but also in terms of structural analysis, that is, how the actions of agents are enabled and constrained by structures.

The concept of system, in the meaning of a totality to be looked at, comes from ancient Greek, but we should not let that trick us into thinking that "system of states" has been a self-referential term for a long time. It is a very recent phenomenon that people who are ruling and administrating states talk about the totality of what they do together in terms of a system. The use of the term began to increase in the first half of the 20th century, and took off after the Second World War. The reason why I would guess this is that "system" is rather new as an analytical term. It hails from the interwar period, and does not really take off in the social sciences until the American sociologist Talcott Parsons became a key name in the 1950s.

In International Relations, the concept of system came into use in the 1960s. It has two principal uses. Let us call them terminological and historical. The terminological use of the concept of system is straightforward. It is to serve as a descriptive catchall, first and foremost for the states system, but also for other relevant systems, such as the global economic system. With one exception, there has been little debate about which system is the more important in IR. The exception is Marxist perspectives. Marxists think of the world first and foremost in terms of means of production and ownership thereto. People relate to one another as a function of their relations to the means of production. For example, in the European Middle Ages, land and tools to work it were the key factor. Humans were defined by their relation to landownership, and humans who shared the same relation to land made up a class. For a Marxist, the key thing for social life is class struggle, be that within or between states. For the Marxist analyst, the key focus is the base, understood as these economically defined relations. Everything that is not base is superstructure. It follows that, to Marxists, the global economic system is more important as an object of study than the states system.

It is analytical use of the term "states system" about historical stuff that is of the essence. We find it among two groups of theorists. The first group is rather small, and concerns itself with which states systems have existed historically. As pointed out in the classic on the issue, Martin Wight's *System of States* (1977), these may be sovereign or suzerain states systems. As noted in chapter 4, suzerainty means that there is one power center around which other polities are subordinated. You will recognize this situation as typical of empires: where there is a strong empire and also certain units that are not formally part of that empire, but whose politics are decisively determined by the existence of a stronger unit, then we have a suzerain system. Historically, there are a number of these. If, on the other hand, units of the system have a high degree of legal and political autonomy from one another, then the units may be said to be sovereign and so may the states system. Sovereign systems may consist of so-called city-states, as did the ancient Greek system or the system that formed in Italy in the 14th and 15th centuries. Then there are a few others. There is, arguably, the so-called Amarna system involving ancient states like Egypt, Hatti, and Alasiya, and then there is the modern states system. One of Wight's followers, Adam Watson (1992), suggested that there is a pendulum movement in world history between suzerain and sovereign periods. This is what we may call a historiosophical speculation. It is stimulating. It is also rather too general, and it is misleading in that a pendulum swings with a certain frequency, whereas sovereign systems pop up stochastically (a social scientist would say that the two phenomena have different temporalities).

Sovereignty and suzerainty are so-called system logics; they tell us something basic about how systems work. Another way of saying this is that a system logic is *structural*.

The Modern States System

The structural logic of the modern states system is sovereign. The question that has exercised a number of scholars is when this system emerged. There is consensus that, given the world's history of imperialism and colonialism, the way to study this is to begin with the emergence of the European states system, and then proceed to study how this system became global. The emergence of states in Europe and the emergence of the system were co-constitutive, which simply means that they created one another. It was not the case that first there were states, and then there was a system. On the contrary, states emerged out of relations between political units that were there before. Drawing on the terminology introduced already, first there was a mediaeval system of suzerain units, and then there was an Early Modern system of sovereign units.

We are talking about a process here, so there are a number of successive steps to consider. One possible starting point, favored by Wight, is the French intervention into the system of Italian city-states in 1494. Another is one of the congresses of states that were called for the purpose of drawing up a peace treaty after long-term hostilities, namely the Congress of Augsburg in 1555. German states had been riddled with conflict between Catholics and Protestants for decades, and a compromise of sorts was reached in the form of *"cuius regio, eius religio,"* which is Latin for "whose realm, his religion" and indicated that each ruler should be able to determine the form of religion to be followed by his subjects. This meant an increase in autonomy, some would argue so large that the German polities went from being a suzerain system under the Holy Roman Empire to being a sovereign system. Others again held that this only happened after the Thirty Years' War, at Westphalia, in 1648. This is actually the orthodox view. It has been much discussed over the last three decades, but we sometimes still hear the modern state described as the Westphalian state, and the modern states system as the Westphalian system.

It may be argued that the modern states system as we know it did not really come into existence before it was further formalized at the Congress of Vienna in 1814–15, but this late dating remains an extreme view. We now turn to the two basic ways of studying the states system, the historical approach and the structural approach.

Historical Approach

In an attempt to get not only at the narrow question of the emergence of the structural logic of sovereignty, but at the wider definitional question of system formalization, Hedley Bull, who was Wight's principal successor, suggested that we could think in terms of when the international system became what he called an international society. International society may be defined as a system where the units—Bull would say members and actually mean states—pay continuous attention to what other states do, and share in the working of common institutions. Since it is only the most abstract system—if indeed there is any—made up of units that are human collectives where the units would not recognize their interactions with other units, the usefulness of the distinction between system and society hinges on institutions. We will return to international society and its institutions in subsequent chapters. For now, let me just note that Alexander Wendt has built on Wight and Bull and suggested three stages of maturity for an international society: Hobbesian, Lockean, and Kantian. You will see that these distinctions simply extend the idea that systems may grow more and more mature, but you will also see that this kind of stage logic has advantages (and disadvantages) when we want to make sense of changes in international interaction.

The question of system maturity should be thought of in combination with the ontic underpinnings for order and hierarchy within states, and anarchy outside, or, if you like, between, states. If we talk about a mature states system, even an international society, then the outside is not anarchic in the sense of having no structure, but only in the technical sense of having no head or leader (from Gr. *an archon*, without head). Bull captured this tension between the regularity needed for there to be something like society on the one hand and the irregularity that follows from there not being any instance from which to enforce that regularity in the title of his 1977 book, *The Anarchical Society*.

Structural Approach

The modern states system may also be approached ahistorically. Let us round off by an example of how to do that, namely so-called structural realism. Realists are not big on the maturing of anarchy. For them, international institutions are epiphenomena, that is, phenomena that have no explanatory power in themselves, because they are derivative of other phenomena. Realists see international institutions as derivative of the states that make up their membership, and as such without much analytical purchase, for states can simply change those institutions at will. To structural realists, then, the states system remains a self-help system regardless of what its institutions look like, and states remain dependent on self-help.

While classical realists focused on statesmen and their actions, so-called neorealism or structural realism focuses on, well, structures. The founder of this school, Kenneth Waltz, understood the states system as consisting of three layers. The basic layer we have already met—it is the question of whether the logic of the system is suzerain or sovereign, or, as Waltz formulates it, whether the basic principle is anarchy or hierarchy. This is what structuralists call the latent structure of the system, the structure that underpins it but that cannot be directly observed. Waltz's second layer concerns what kinds of units will be generated by the latent structure. The point here is that anarchy *by necessity* will generate polities that are "like units"—meaning simply that they are all of the same kind, all like one another. The reason is simple: anarchy is a self-help system, which means that, in order to survive, the units will have to imitate one another's innovations to survive. Those units that do not will disappear, and so an anarchic system will have like units. In the case of the modern states system, those will be states. This means that it is only the third and observable or manifest layer of the system where there can be any change. This layer concerns the relative strength of states, and so this, and this only, becomes the focus of structural realist analysis. Consequently, structural realism discusses things like how long today's system will remain unipolar (Brooks and Wohlforth 2008; see also Deudney 2008).

Structural realism is what we call a structural functionalist way of analyzing the states system. It was drawn up to understand the Cold War system, and cannot explain why the Cold War came to an end, or any other systemic change for that matter. What it can do is help us think through the logic of anarchy. A historical approach like that discussing maturity and an ahistorical approach like structuralism may be at loggerheads, but they both offer approaches that you can draw on to understand the system.

Key Questions

Are states systems the historical rule?

What does it mean to say that anarchy can mature?

Note

1. For a historical walkthrough of institutional thought in the social sciences, see Scott 2008, chapters 1 and 2.

Bibliography

Albert, Mathias, Lars-Erik Cederman, and Alexander Wendt, eds. 2010. *New Systems Theories of World Politics*. Basingstoke: Palgrave.

Brooks, Stephen G., and William C. Wohlforth. 2008. *World Out of Balance: International Relations and the Challenge of American Primacy*. Princeton: Princeton University Press.

Deudney, Daniel H. 2008. *Bounding Power: Republican Security Theory from the Polis to the Global Village*. Princeton: Princeton University Press.

Scott, Richard W. 2008. *Institutions and Organizations: Ideas, Interests and Identities*. London: Sage.

Waltz, Kenneth. 1979. *Theory of International Politics*. Toronto: Addison-Wesley.

Watson, Adam. 1992. *The Evolution of International Society: A Comparative Historical Analysis*. London: Routledge.

Wendt, Alexander. 1999. *Social Theory of International Politics*. Cambridge: Cambridge University Press.

Wight, Martin. 1977. *System of States*. Leicester: Leicester University Press.

Eugène Delacroix's *La liberté guidant le peuple* (Freedom guides the people, 1830) is one of the most famous examples of the by now global practice of anthropomorphizing the nation. (Courtesy Wikimedia Commons)

8 ✦ Nationalism, Postcolonialism, and Euro-Centrism

This chapter introduces three concepts that ground specific literatures. It will nonetheless be beneficial to link them. Nationalism is a political doctrine, which holds that the world is divided into nations, and that those who belong to a nation should also make up a state. Holding that the world consists of this, that, or the other thing is an ontic claim. Early nation builders made the ontic claim that nations were physiologically, psychologically, and socially real, and had always been real, but that they had been dormant through long periods of time. The job of the nation builders was to awaken them. The nationalist doctrine is that the boundaries of the nation and the boundaries of the state should be contiguous. Postcolonialism is also first and foremost an ontic term, referring to the social and political state of things following the end of formal imperialism in the decades after the Second World War. Our third concept, Euro-centrism, is first and foremost an epistemological term (to do with how we know), referring to practices of privileging the role of Europe over the role of other continents and over global *problematiques*. In conclusion, I discuss how the three are linked.

Nationalism

We already met nationalism in chapter 3, as the doctrine of self-determination: a group that is a nation, that is, which is a cultural entity, should also be a political entity. What is a cultural entity according to nationalism? Language and religion are key markers, but there are others. The key thing is difference from other groups. Things that are not only different, but considered both (a) different and (b) of political importance by the group itself are key. So, speaking about key, singing in unison and in public was a key marker of Estonian and Latvian nationality in the late

1980s and early 1990s, when these two nations were very active in trying to break out of the Soviet Union.

There is a sense in which the idea that culture is relevant to politics may be traced way back in history, in the sense that small hunter-gatherer bands know all other members of the group personally. Many people, for example the Inuit, have a name for themselves that translates as "human," implying that everybody else is something else. With increasing complexity, this changed. The ancient Greeks did tend to lump everybody that did not speak Greek together as barbarians—those who bleated *bar bar* instead of speaking properly. Despite this rather animal-like categorization, however, there was no longer any question that barbarians were humans. That is historically very important indeed. In the Roman Empire, the key distinction was not ethnic, but whether or not you were a Roman citizen. The concept of "nation" traces back to Latin *natio*, which comes from being born (compare "nascent"), and underlines that we are talking about common origins, or kinship. In the Middle Ages, "nation" was used about groups of students or traders that were born in the same places but congregated in another. The key thing to note here is that a nation was indeed a polity—recall that having we-ness is one of three defining traits of a polity (with the other two being mustering of resources and a degree of hierarchy), but that it was a peripheral kind of polity.

With the coming of Protestantism in Europe, one specific trait, namely difference in religion, became key to political life. There had been lots of religious fallings out before that—Sunni versus Shia and Christian Orthodox vs. Catholics to mention but two biggies—but that happened in the context of empire. With Protestantism, the singling out of a cultural trait as a political marker began to coincide with state building.

So much for the prehistory. The proper history of nationalism starts in the late 18th century, in Germany, within that period that German conceptual historian Reinhart Koselleck singles out as "the saddle time" (Ger. *Die Sattelzeit*)—the transitional period leading to our own time (1750–1850). German speakers were spread out across empires, states, and city-states when thinkers such as Johann Georg Hamann, Johann Gottfried Herder, and Johann Gottlieb Fichte began to speak about the nation. Nationalism, the doctrine that states and nations should coincide, was also a celebration of the peasant and the simple man, and so this new Romanticism stood in stark opposition to Enlightenment thinking, which celebrated the educated (read: the bourgeois) and civilization. And here a specific culture (German, but also Italian, and so forth) was an alternative to (French) civilization.

Why nationalism? The emergence of nationalism coincides with the beginnings of the grand movement of people from the countryside to the city. In the city, there was no immediate community. One reading of national is as a family writ large, a simulated family to replace the village left behind. Other readings stress the importance of printing; once books became available in the vernacular, an important factor of communication exerted pressure on political life.

Nationalism was hugely successful in the 19th century. In the late 19th and early 20th century, it was challenged by Marxism, which held that class, not nation, was the key group that should attract peoples' allegiances. Nationalism won a decisive victory over Marxism, which is to say that the concept of "nation" proved more fundamental than the concept of "class," when, at the outbreak of the Great War in 1914, socialists everywhere sided with their national governments, rather than with their comrades abroad. The exception was Russia, where socialist internationalism seemingly held sway as the Soviet Union emerged. However, nationalism soon snuck up on Soviet communism, too, and nationalism was a factor in the 1991 end of the Soviet Union. From the 1970s onward, nationalism has been challenged by globalization, which is the topic of the following chapter (Bartelson 2009).

Postcolonialism

"Post" simply means "after" in Latin, so postcolonialism is that which comes after colonialism. Colonialism is the process of making colonies out of something that was not a colony before, with colony being a periphery of an empire. But why the "ism"? Because postcolonialism refers not simply to what comes after colonies, but to the state of being a postcolonial state—a postcolony, as it were—or being a postcolonial subject. Note, then, that postcolonialism is a global concept, for being a postcolonial subject is not tied to any specific territory; you can do it in Accra, you can do it in London, and you can do it in Ulaanbaatar.

It could be argued that, with globalization, we all become postcolonial subjects, for we are all affected by the breakup of empires, which has meant the intensification of flows of people, ideas, and so forth throughout the world. In this broad sense, postcolonialism is nothing less than a bid for describing what it is like to be a human in the world these days. Postcolonialism is nonetheless usually used in a narrower form, about being a subject from a postcolony, someone who has a mental experience of being at the receiving end of (post)colonialism. It is not only a temporal term, about what comes after empire, but also an ontic term, which refers to a state of being. Note, for example, the book title *On the Postcolony* (2001). For Achille Mbembe, the author, his native Cameroon is a postcolony, where one leads a postcolonial existence, but Mbembe also holds that he himself has led a postcolonial existence when he studied in Paris and is still doing so when he is working in South Africa.

In Western discourse, the concept of neocolonialism was often used in the 1970s. It focused on how Western structures, notably capitalism, perpetuated global structures such as unequal trade, which kept former colonies in an unprivileged and dependent position. The so-called dependency theorists—Andre Gunder Frank (German American, 1929–2005), Samir Amin (Egyptian 1931–), and later Brazilian president Fernando Henrique Cardoso (1931–)—were the key theorists of neocolonialism. Whereas neocolonialism was a Marxist-inspired mode of social analysis, focusing on economic issues, postcolonialism is more existentialist and focuses on social and political life in general. Postcolonialism has certain Marxist roots, but it is not itself Marxist. Let me be more specific. Marxism holds that productive forces define humans, and that the play of productive forces—economics—are the base of society, while everything else is superstructure. A number of postcolonialists would disagree with that, and focus on human consciousness and the experience of having been at the receiving end of colonialism as the key phenomenon rather than economics.

The foundational works of postcolonialism are *The Wretched of the Earth* ([1961] 2004) by Franz Fanon and *Orientalism* (1978) by Edward Said. Since human experience is at the heart of the matter for a postcolonialist, minibiographies are warranted. Fanon (1925–61) was born in Martinique, which is an overseas part of France in the Caribbean, trained in France as a doctor, worked in Algeria, and traveled across the French Empire. He was a typical product of empire. *The Wretched of the Earth* is a study in racism and alienation and is the key work documenting how people working for decolonization thought about the plight of the world, and their own plight in it. The book has a preface by the French Marxist philosopher Jean-Paul Sartre, which glorifies violence. It is important to note that Fanon died before he could do anything about it being printed, and that commissioning it was the publisher's idea in the first place. Given that the preface is wholly out of tune with the book, it seems unlikely that Sartre actually read the book before writing its preface. It would, therefore, be unwarranted to argue that Fanon glorifies violence on the grounds that the preface to his key book does so (Bhabha 2004).

Edward Said (1935–2003) was a Christian Arab Palestinian who grew up in Jerusalem and Cairo and spent his working life at Columbia University in New York. *Orientalism* (1978) focuses on how specific patterns of thought about the other as inferior have the effect of perpetuating that inferiority. Said's case is scholarly representations of the Orient, hence the book's title. *Orientalism* has been enormously influential as a sensitizing device for how the Middle East has been represented in Europe and the United States, and for the importance of representations to political life generally. Said has been criticized for his emphasis on the Middle East— what about Middle Eastern Occidentalist representations of the West or Ottoman and Turkish Orientalist representations of Arabs, as discussed in chapter 3?—and for totalizing the historical period about which he writes, which is two millennia long, whereas formal colonialism lasted less than two centuries. It is true that representations of the Other are generally quite hairy; if we look at how Chinese and Europeans represented one another in the late Middle Ages, for example, we find that both parties saw the other as subhuman, with eyes on their stomachs, no neck, and so forth. The key point about *Orientalism* for IR is that it revitalized the study of how representations are central to political relations between polities.

The basic idea is that "the East" is a constitutive outside for "the West," which means that the East is the Other from which the West has to limit, or limn, its identity. Identity demands difference to be, and turns difference into Otherness in order to secure itself. Epistemologically, Said places the terrain on which this happens not in the psychic system, where many scholars had placed it previously, but in the social system. It is the *social* representations of the Other, and not the mental constructs thereof, that are of the essence.

Although Said, who was trained as a literary critic, investigated a number of genres, he singles out one particular genre, namely scientific writing, as particularly important. This is in keeping with Said's leading theoretical light, the poststructuralist Michel Foucault, and his understanding of what

Foucault calls the power/knowledge nexus. Power/knowledge is a single entity. Knowledge, as a representational system, is about producing social reality. This means that representation is productive—that is, it has social effects. As a particularly cherished representational system, scientific knowledge is particularly productive and powerful.

Said's book *Orientalism* is what we may call self-referentially successful. It argues that scientific texts may be powerful by changing social reality, and the book has done exactly that. In scientific discourse, Orientalism now refers to the kind of subordinating Othering of "Easterners" by "Westerners" that the book critiques. There is a knock-on effect on political discourse, where the scientific debunking of Orientalism serves as a power resource for those who strive to counteract the kind of Western identity building that involves bashing postcolonies.

A third key postcolonial force that should be mentioned in addition to Fanon and Said is the Calcutta subaltern historians. They combine an epistemological project, namely excavating subaltern life during colonial times, with an ontic one, which is validating subaltern being and agency in the world.

What is the relationship between nationalism and postcolonialism? To repeat, nationalism is a political doctrine, which lays down that a nation—whatever that may be—should have a state. One way of thinking about the end of Western empires is that they were overthrown by the idea of nationalism, for empires by definition consist of a number of nations, and so are antithetical to the doctrine of nationalism. Postcolonies—what comes after imperial colonies—are empirically the new nation-states in Africa and Asia that emerged after the Second World War. Postcolonialism can then be understood as the remnants of empire; in an institutional sense, the remnants of political control, and in a mental sense, the remnants of feeling controlled by or, to use a postcolonial term, subaltern to former colonial masters. Where nationalism is supposed to denote an active political being-in-the-world, postcolonialism is supposed to denote a passive political being-in-the-world. To many postcolonial writers, nationalism was the promise, but postcolonialism turned out to be the result.

Euro-Centrism

We have talked about nationalism and postcolonialism as political terms denoting programs and beings-in-the-world. By contrast, according to John

M. Hobson (2004, 2), Euro-centrism is "the notion that the West properly deserves to occupy the centre stage of progressive world history, both past and present." Euro-centrism seems to be a fairly new concept. The oldest reference I have found is from 1914 (Witte 1914). It is an epistemological concept, relating to how we try to understand the world and how we produce knowledge about it. The basic idea here is that ruling thoughts are the thoughts of the rulers. Europe dominated global knowledge production in the period 1800–1950. The European educational system, founded on schools and universities with a broad curriculum, spread, and brought European ways of thinking about the world with it. This happened to the detriment of other ways of producing and organizing knowledge. We may observe this phenomenon at all levels of intellectual life. For example, the leading global genres of writing—the essay, the monograph, the paper, and the novel—are all Western forms. Most leading institutions are Western institutions, and those that are not Western, in the sense of being located in the West, are still modeled on Western institutions. Note that I slip from European to Western here. When we speak about the world after the Second World War and formal imperialism, it makes little sense to say that it was a European-led world. Given the rise of a European settler colony, the United States, to global leadership, however, Euro-centrism was perpetuated as it were by proxy, and this we may denote by talking about Western rather than European hegemony.

In 2000, Dipesh Chakrabarty published a book called *Provincialising Europe*. In the first chapter, he formulates what has become known as Chakrabarty's problem, which is this: How should a postcolonial scholar analyze the world? If the analysis starts from Western concepts, the analysis will reproduce the Western knowledge regime. On the other hand, if the scholar starts from a local, say Hindi, knowledge regime, then global realities may be very hard to catch. I can see no answer to this dilemma. It is the same dilemma that the Indian philosopher Gayatri Chakravorty Spivak addressed when she called a review of the Calcutta-based subaltern historians "Can the Subaltern Speak?" (1988) and answered in the negative. The subaltern cannot speak because she does not have her own language to speak in. This is, of course, an answer that takes some of its fizz from being hyperbolic. Subalterns can speak, but not fully in their own voice. The big postcolonial names—Edward Said, Homi Bhabha, Gayatri Chakravorty Spivak, Achille Mbembe, Mahmood Mamdani—were all educated at Western universities, as are most postcolonial scholars. So, at the level of which concepts we use, all present-day academics are more or less Euro-centric.

What we can do is to be self-reflective about this. At the level of topics that we choose to study, it is much easier to combat Euro-centrism, for we can do it by directing our efforts to non-European topics.

One interesting take on how European institutions spread that should be mentioned here comes from John W. Meyer and the so-called Stanford school of sociology. Their basic claim is that, on the one hand, the spread of Western forms makes the world an increasingly homogeneous place, for it ensures isomorphism, that is, likeness of form, in world society. Take universities; they tend to be similar the world over. Traffic regulation has moved and is moving in the same direction. On the other hand, the content of these similar institutions remain different. History syllabi at different universities vary with what kind of national and other history is being taught and researched. In some countries, traffic regulation regulates left-hand driving, in others, right-hand driving. The form is similar, and similar form shapes content, but content nonetheless remains different.

Most institutions in global politics—diplomacy and the balance of power are key examples—have their major (but not their only) origins in European traditions, and have then spread. In order to understand global politics, then, there is no way around privileging these institutions when we study IR. If the global institutions are modeled primarily on European ones, and we are supposed to study global institutions, then we are looking at a structurally inevitable Euro-centrism. The knowledge output will reflect this Euro-centrism. But that's not the end of the story. There are various ways of changing this—research focus, new epistemologies and forms of inquiry, training people from backgrounds who have not traditionally been tied in to the university tradition, including discussions of Eurocentrism in textbooks, and working at self-awareness.

Relations

In terms of ontology, nationalism is an ingredient in the struggle against colonialism. The doctrine of self-determination laid down that nations in the colonies should throw off the imperial yoke and form their own states. Self-determination is simply the doctrine of nationalism spelled out in a colonial context: a national self is entitled to determine how it should be ruled, and, to a nationalist, that means forming a state. The ontological claim concerns contiguity of state and nation, and comes to the fore when it is argued that it is "natural" that this or that minority is eliminated (by assimilation, exile, or extermination, or a combination of the three) or that this or that minority in one nation-state whose fellow nationals form a majority in some other nation-state, a so-called diaspora, is "brought home."

Postcolonialism is also basically an ontic term, for it describes a way of being-in-the-world. However, where the focus of nationalism is institutional—how to build a nation-state—postcolonialism's focus is mental—it tries to describe a social and individual mentality. It tries to pinpoint what some specific being-in-the-world *is like*.

In this focus on the mental, on social psychology, if you like, postcolonialism is akin to Euro-centrism, which is an epistemological term. Where postcolonialism denotes what it is like being-in-the-world, Euro-centrism denotes one way of orienting oneself in the world, namely by privileging European experiences and ways of producing knowledge. I think we are warranted in saying that what makes postcolonial subjects postcolonial subjects is exactly that they constantly have to grapple with Euro-centrism. In order to go on in the world, they somehow have to reconcile a European-inspired way of thinking with some other tradition's way of thinking, knowing full well that that other tradition has been historically marginalized by the European tradition. And it is this fact, that a majority of the world's population, and to an increasing degree everybody, has to grapple with these dilemmas, that is the reason why some of us think that cultural hybridization is a key characteristic of today's world.

Key Questions

To what extent does the nationalization of the state prevent the imaginary of different kinds of community?

Is Euro-centrism in International Relations inevitable?

Bibliography

Bartelson, Jens. 2009. *Visions of World Community*. Cambridge: Cambridge University Press.

Bhabha, Homi K. 2004. "Foreword: Framing Fanon." In Franz Fanon's *The Wretched of the Earth*, vii–xli. New York: Grove Press.

Chakrabarty, Dipesh. 2000. *Provincialising Europe: Post-Colonial Thought and Historical Difference*. Princeton: Princeton University Press.

Fanon, Franz. [1961] 2004. *The Wretched of the Earth*. New York: Grove Press.

Hobson, John. 2004. *The Eastern Origins of Western Civilization*. Cambridge: Cambridge University Press.

Mbembe, Achille. 2001. *On the Postcolony*. Berkeley: University of California Press.

Said, Edward. 1978. *Orientalism*. London: Penguin.

Spivak, Gayatri Chakravorty. 1988. "Can the Subaltern Speak?" In *Marxism and the Interpretation of Culture*, ed. Cary Nelson and Lawrence Grossberg, 271–316. Urbana: University of Illinois Press.

Witte, Johannes. 1914. *Ostasien und Europa: Das Ringen zweier Weltkulturen*. Tübingen: J.C.B. Mohr.

9 ✦ Globalization and Global Governance

What is the proper object of study of IR? Some of the answers given above are agentic, and some are structural. The key candidate for a structural concept at the heart of the discipline so far has been the states system, but there are others as well, such as the economic system. Following a quick look at "the international," this chapter will look at two structural concepts that seem to challenge the states system as our primary object of study, namely globalization and global governance.

"The international" is not at loggerheads with the states system, but simply pertains to what is going on between nations, in the sense of states. The key thing to note about the international is that it embraces not only state-to-state relations but also all other relations between agents that are based in different states. A gathering of, say, lawyers is international if it harbors lawyers from more than one state. When we add the suffix "ism" to an adjective and make it a noun, we make it into an ideological phenomenon, and so internationalism is about somehow celebrating the international.

The global typically refers to a social reality that is geographically more wide-reaching than the international—a gathering of Asian dentists or European lawyers is definitely international, but it is not global. If we add the suffix "ization" to an adjective, we do so to capture a process. It is a way of characterizing a temporal sequence (with temporality being the way time manifests itself in human existence; Hoy 2009). The legal is what pertains to the law; legalization is the formalizing process that turns stuff that was formerly simply norm-setting into law. By the same token, globalization is a concept that is meant to capture the intensification of ever more global flows of people, ideas, goods, and services.

Finally, global governance is simply systems of informal rule that are meant to be global in reach. Global governance arises when state rule, state governance, and international treaties are not deemed to be enough to regulate and order an emergent social reality. An increase in global governance may be an intended or an unintended occurrence.

As you will see, all these terms arose as tentative answers to the emergent problem of more human interaction at farther distances and across state boundaries. They are attempts to capture no less than the question of how social interaction in the world is changing.

The International

"International" is a concept suggested by Jeremy Bentham in his 1789 *Introduction to the Principles of Morals and Legislation*, as he clarified in a footnote:

> The word international, it must be acknowledged, is a new one; though, it is hoped, sufficiently analogous and intelligible. It is calculated to express, in a more significant way, the branch of law, which goes commonly under the name of the law of nations. (Bentham [1823] 1907, 326)

"The international" thus started life as a legal and residual category; it is what is left of law once we have considered national law. The term then widened to include nonlegal stuff as well.

Internationalism, an ideological celebration of the process of internationalization, came into use a century or so later, finding perhaps its most prominent expression in the writings of the British peace activist Norman Angell (1872–1967). Angell began to write in the years before the Great War of 1914–18, and his main concern was to forge links between groups of people in different states in order to avoid an international confrontation. He did not succeed, and after the First World War he continued his work, now centering on the new international organization of the day, the League of Nations. His thoughts spread throughout Northern Europe. For example, in 1925, Christian Lous Lange received the Nobel Peace Prize for his work as secretary general of the Inter-Parliamentary Union, a forum for European parliamentarians that still exists. Lange is also the author of a three-volume work on internationalism, by which he meant the political doctrine that states should live in peace with one another, as well as the work that was going into reaching that peaceful state of affairs. What little there is of theoretical thought in Lange's historical work is drawn from Angell.

Note that Angell's work was propelled by an observable change in social patterns: at the end of the 19th century, the density of relations between groups in different states, be that concerning trade, services, political activity, or intellectual work, was all rapidly increasing. It has been largely forgotten today, but the decade before the Great War was also the age when people campaigned for doing away with international legitimation papers, and so for opening the world to the free movement of people. That did not materialize, but, after the turmoil of the interwar period and the Second World War, the founding of the United Nations once again fueled internationalism. Internationalists gathered in support of the United Nations, just as Angell and others had forged the League of Nations so that citizens of different countries could work in unison to support that international organization.

Globalization

A globe—the word hails from the late Middle Ages—is a sphere, and global simply means spherical. The use of "globe" about planet Earth arose in the 16th century, at the same time as the known world expanded from one to many continents, and global in the sense of planet-wide only hails from the end of the 19th century, as the globe had indeed become one and shrunk, at least as seen from the point of view of the industrialized world.

Internationalization can be defined as an increase in density of relations between groups (or even things) that are representative of states, where the key thing is that these groups are conceived of as being distinctly national—that is, somehow representative of the state from which they hail. Globalization is a deeper social phenomenon, referring to the increased density of social relations across the world. The point is no longer simply that groups that meet are representative of certain states. That is no longer their "imperative status," to use a sociological term. It is not that citizenship and cultural knowledge of a specific state becomes irrelevant, but these things no longer dominate the interactions. The interactions are in a higher degree detached from the state-to-state logic that characterized them under conditions of internationalization.

An everyday example would be food. Food is what an anthropologist would call a total social fact—it seeps through the entire social fabric and is impossible to avoid, for obvious biological reasons. When I was a boy, we sometimes had an Indian or a Chinese meal, but that always happened in a specially designated space—in an Indian or Chinese restaurant (which were both new phenomena in Oslo, Norway)—and it always marked a special time (something should be celebrated or the day should be marked as special for other reasons). It was, if you like, an "international" experience—"the Chinese" remained clearly separated from "the Norwegian." Now, compare that to the Thai experience of developing Thai food since the coming of the British in the 19th century. Siam and then Thailand incorporated elements of other food traditions into Thai cuisine. Today, it is probably not all that interesting to ask where the different elements hailed from in the first place, for the result is something new. Thai cuisine has become *hybridized*: it is characterized by how a lot of borrowed elements have resulted in a new phenomenon. It then spread to the rest of the world, where it is becoming even further hybridized. The same point may be made about most cuisines of this world. This hybridization goes beyond an internationalization of food, for the point is not only that the first course hails from place A, the second course from place B, and the pudding from place C. It is rather that food everywhere is being globalized. I am of course using food here as an example of a social phenomenon that can stand in for social interaction in its entirety. Social life as such has undergone a process of hybridization. This is particularly obvious in world cities like Paris or Rio de Janeiro.

So, globalization is different from internationalization in that interactions are no longer experienced as between states or between groups within states, but rather as interactions between groups that may, or may not, be seen as national in the context of those interactions.

Globalization has two preconditions, infrastructure and technology. It is common to speak about globalization as a changing of time-space, in the sense that the world shrinks. Stuff—be that persons, goods, or communications—takes a shorter time to get from A to B. There is a change in temporality. This bleeds into a changing of space, since two sites that are quickly reached from one another will have the potential to become closer socially. I say will have the potential to, for other factors may intervene; go by car for a couple of hours from any capital in the world, and you will find pockets of people who commute to the capital every day. You will also find other pockets of people, however, who almost never travel to the capital. Short travel distances enable a compression of space, but there may be intervening factors that constrain such compression from happening.

Globalization was also greatly eased by the end of empire, which meant that political forces geared toward keeping stuff in one place were eased. Globalization is a key phenomenon for IR, because it changes the social situation within which state relations take place. The new situation increases the importance of questions like the importance of states and the states system relative to other actors. We see this in scientific discourse concerning the central *object* to be studied: global studies vs. "International" Relations. If you hark back to the previous chapter and its discussion of postcolonialism, you will see that it is globalization that makes postcolonialism into more than a local phenomenon in a postcolony.

When, how, and why did globalization come to be experienced as a problem by large numbers of people? We need a study of how this happened, for, after the end of the Cold War (1947–89), it seems that whether one celebrates or rejects globalization has become a key political divide in most of the world. One way of reading the resurgence of populism and nationalism in places like India (Hindutva), Turkey (Islamists), the United Kingdom (Brexit), and the United States (Donald Trump) is as reactions against the arrival of the global, with all its difference and variety.

Global Governance

With more and more stuff happening along other axes than bilaterally between states—that is, with increasing globalization—how is order maintained? Since its rise some 30 years ago, "global governance" has been the term of choice for this *problematique*. American IR scholar James Rosenau coined the term in a 1992 book, and you get a rough idea about what he had in mind from the title of the book that launched the term: *Governance without Government: Order and Change in World Politics*. Governance, an older concept, means steering, governing. Government governs; the overall term for that process is "governance." The basic opposition is between ruling, that is commanding ("Thou shalt"), on the one hand, and governing (let's talk about this and find a way), on the other. In IR, global governance tends to refer to governing in which states are joined by other agents, or where transnational governance happens without states. The phenomenon has ancient roots, one of which is a body of law known as *lex mercatoria*, a trader-evolved code of conduct that is a forerunner of what is now called international private law.

To a discipline that is dominated by state-centric theorizing, it has become increasingly difficult to explain governance that is not conducted by states. Thus a central problem to be addressed by all schools of thought is to explain the phenomenon of global governance. Let us turn to three bodies of general theorizing—constructivism/liberalism, realism, and poststructuralism—for answers.

First, a constructivist take. Constructivists are interested in how norms, understood as standards for appropriate behaviour—what is considered normal, as it were—spread throughout the world. The first institutionalized example is probably British missionaries, and particularly their wives, campaigning against Chinese foot-binding (see note 1 in chapter 5). Constructivists tend to see a growth of global sensibilities; things increasingly become common concerns. It is apposite to note here that activist activity commences at about the same time as public outrage against something that not only happens in one's own state or its immediate neighborhood, but also to strangers. This is a relatively new phenomenon. A very early example is what is referred to as "the Bulgarian horrors" in English, namely the crushing of the Bulgarian April Uprising of 1876 against the Ottoman Empire. Eyewitnesses reported that Ottoman soldiers bayoneted people in the thousands, children included, and an outcry arose throughout Europe and the United States. It has become a sign of the times that global campaigns target what are seen as inhumane practices, in increasingly local places. One example is the campaigns and public outcry in a number of places across the globe against cultural practices like the annual traditional whale hunt in the Faeroe Island (pop. 30,000). The favorite, and perhaps best, example given by constructivists is not particularist, however, but ostensibly universal, namely human rights. Constructivists see human rights widen and deepen as a spiral, which also demarcates a sphere where states have to stoop to international norms. Norms go on to become law. A central problem remains, however: Are human rights something that is guaranteed by states, as argue, for example, the Chinese and Russian states, or are they something above the state that has to be left to supranational, that is, suprastate, organs, like international courts of law? Well, if human rights are really about universal human rights, as opposed to the rights of state subjects, then they logically have to be above states, and so cannot be left to states to implement. Human rights can only be protected, constructivists claim, by something that stands above the state, and their favorite candidate is not a world state, but international law.

To this constructivist take on global governance, we may juxtapose a realist take. To realists, global governance is an epiphenomenon, that is, a phenomenon that explains nothing, but that is itself explained by something else. Interdependence between states and international law, realists maintain, do not really constrain states, for when it comes right down to it, states can do what they want. To a realist, interdependence is like a cobweb covering the mouth of a cannon. If the state wants to, it can fire its cannons, the *ultima ratio regis* (Lat., the king's ultimate argument), and interdependence is gone. Global governance therefore needs no explanation, because it does not exist in the first place. Here you might want to object: but global governance *is* observable in a number of settings. Well, yes, realists would say, but not where it counts, which is in high politics, in national security. And where it seems to exist, realists would argue, it is just allowed to exist by states that have delegated to other actors to dabble in details. The state remains the principal actor, the one that can simply withdraw the authority it has delegated at any time if it so wishes.

When a scholar is faced with two opposite theoretical perspectives, one possible answer is to attempt a third reading that incorporates elements of them both. That is what Ole Jacob Sending and I attempted with constructivist and realist views on global governance in our book *Governing the Global Polity* (Neumann and Sending 2010). We argued that realists are right in charging constructivists with neglecting power. Norms are too thin an explanation for such a pervasive and world-historical phenomenon as globalization, for norms ride on the back of power. On the other hand, we argued that realists are wrong to argue that there has been no change in governing practices, and that states have simply gone on acting like they always have. Empirically, that is simply not the case. States have vastly larger action capacity today than they had a century ago, they have a lot more interfaces with society, and they have a whole series of new ways of operating in the world. Constructivists are right that culture and identity are important factors, and so constructivists are the ones that can specify our understanding of change, while realists simply repeat the antihistorical argument that a state is a state is a state.

We may reconcile the two by leaning on the poststructuralist idea that states govern *through* groups and individuals. They do this by intentionally and unintentionally manipulating knowledge (norms, rules, how we think in general). Consider the work done by, say, a development NGO or an IO like the World Bank. Their personnel tends to think very similarly, that is, they tend to lean on and reproduce knowledge that celebrates a specific kind of world order. What we are talking about here is indeed a spread of norms, just as constructivists argue, but this spread of norms is shot through with a specific form of power that we will discuss at length in chapter 17, namely governmentality. Realists are therefore right to stress the continued importance of power to global life. States that depend heavily on governmentality, however, are rather different creatures than states that avail themselves primarily of other forms of power, and so realists are wrong to argue that globalization does not change the state.[1]

To sum up, as pointed out by Jens Bartelson (2006), we might see the rise of a global society as a result of global governance, governed into existence as an object of governance. This is not to say that states cease to exist or that they become irrelevant—states remain important. In some ways, they may even increase in importance. The point, though, is that they do so by working *through* other agents.

Key Questions

Is the world becoming more internationalized, more globalized, both, or neither?

Is global governance just a way in which the West governs the rest?

Note

1. For a discussion of power and governmentality, see chapter 17.

Bibliography

Bartelson, Jens. 2006. "Making Sense of Global Civil Society." *European Journal of International Relations* 12 (3): 371–95.

Bentham, Jeremy. [1823] 1907. *The Principles of Morals and Legislation*. Oxford: Clarendon.

Goldmann, Kjell. 1994. *The Logic of Internationalism: Coercion and Accommodation*. London: Routledge.

Hoy, David Couzens. 2009. *The Time of Our Lives: A Critical History of Temporality*. Cambridge, MA: MIT Press.

Neumann, Iver B., and Ole Jacob Sending. 2010. *Governing the Global Polity: Practice, Rationality, Mentality*. Ann Arbor: University of Michigan Press.

Rosenau, James N., and Ernst-Otto Czempiel, eds. 1992. *Governance without Government: Order and Change in World Politics*. Cambridge: Cambridge University Press.

10 ✦ Security

Concepts of security	Period
Individual security	Ancient
Collective security	Classical
State security	Modern
Discursive security	Postmodern

In Latin, *securus* means without care and *securitas* refers to the state of being free from care. So, how did the state of being carefree or even careless transmute into security in the English language?

It did not happen immediately. William Shakespeare, the person who did perhaps most to shape Modern English as we know it, has Macbeth (act 3, scene 5) use the concept in the sense of carelessness: "securitee is mortals' cheefest enemy." This meaning dropped away. Instead, we were left with a bifurcation of the concept of "security" into one usage for individuals and one for polities. When used about individuals, "security" came to refer to what we often call safety, and the means to get there are usually understood as building fences, buying keys, installing surveillance cameras, and the like. A huge industry has come to cater to this sort of thing. The two principal firms, both hailing from a firm formed by two Danish brothers in the 1960s, are G4S and, yes, Securitas (Abrahamsen and Williams 2010).

By contrast, where polities are concerned, security came to mean not only immediate physical safety but also everything that concerns who should be secure against what, by which means, how. There is a literature on how the meaning of security understood as personal safety and security understood as state security now merge, so that firms like G4S offer private security services that may stand in for, or even be bought by, states, but IR is particularly interested in the second term, which came to denote *the security of a polity*. For some time now, that polity or collective has usually been the state.

Collective Security

Usually, but not exclusively. If we put the two words collective and security together, we may end up with the security of a collective, with the collective being the state, but we may also end up with collective security for a *group* of states. "Collective security" is a concept that has been floated almost throughout the states system's existence, and refers not to the idea of security for one specific state, but to security for many states working together. The basic idea is that if all units in a system guarantee one another's security, then there will be security for all units. The League of Nations was, among other things, an attempt at achieving such a situation. It failed. There are a number of reasons why, but I want you to consider a general problem with collective action, and hence collective security, that has to do with the nature of alliances. It is known as the stag hunt, and was first suggested by Jean-Jacques Rousseau in the *Discourse on the Origins of Inequality* (1754).[1] It was introduced into IR by Kenneth Waltz in *Man, the State, and War* (1959). Rousseau actually used the idea of the stag hunt to describe the transcendence of individual or "infant" man into a social being, so that the stag hunt was all about language and how to negotiate an outcome that was nice for the common good. Waltz took Rousseau's two sentences about the stag hunt in that book, spliced it with game theory and came up with what is in effect a new usage, which goes like this:

A group of hunters have decided to go stag hunting, in the hope of securing meat for themselves and their families. They take cover at the edge of a wood, overlooking a glen. Before long, a hare comes hopping. The first hunter knows that if he shoots the hare, he will have enough meat for himself and his family. He also knows that if he shoots the hare, the ensuing commotion will scare off any stag, and so his shooting the hare will put paid to the mutually decided and cooperative goal for the hunt, which was to kill a stag. That will mean that all the other hunters and their families will probably go hungry that day. On the other hand, he has to take into consideration that, were he not to shoot the hare, the next hunter might, and then he and his own family would have to go without food. In order for the stag hunt still to be on, each and every hunter would have to refrain from shooting the hare that hops right under their noses. This little parable captures the key problems in getting people to act collectively—how it may be hard to forego gains for yourself, even when that will destroy an alliance (such as a shooting party), and how each unit in a system will fear that the others will break ranks.

The stag hunt captures some of the dilemmas of collective action (with the major omission being the problem of free riders). It is sometimes used to argue that it is impossible to form lasting alliances. Baruch Spinoza was the first to argue this way, when he held that once the danger against which an alliance is formed is over or the gain the alliance was formed to make is in hand, the alliance would evaporate.

State Security

Let us now turn to state security. Who seeks security, against whom or what, with which means, and when? As to who seeks security, we have already noted that the unit may be an individual. One may seek security against natural disasters, such as floods or, perhaps in the not so distant future, incoming meteorites. We have also noted that the means may be cooperation between units. Within the states system, however, it is usually assumed that the key logic concerns how states seek security against one another.

I have already indicated repeatedly why this is so. An assumption is often made that the states system is anarchic, which means that it has no ruler. An anarchic system is a self-help system—when the shit hits the fan, no one or no thing may help you other than yourself. In such a system, each unit will look out for its own security. There are two principal ways of doing this, and when taken together, these two principal ways answer the question of what to build security with. The first one is to build defenses, and the second one is to build weapons and the skills to use them.

First, defenses. Think about the long mounds of mud that sedentary populations along the rim of the Eurasian steppe dug up as defense against the nomads' horses (some of which grew to become the Great Wall of China), or the forts of mediaeval Europe, or the drawbridges that we may find all over the world. The goal here is what security scholars call denial, that is, to deny an enemy access.

Second, weapons and skills. Producing more weapons may increase security. So may improving already known weapons and inventing new ones. Just as important is the building of individual skills in using them, plans for how to use them—such plans are called tactics when they concern how to reach specific goals like winning a battle and strategy when they concern reaching more complex goals like winning a war and the peace that follows it—and organizations that may use the weapons.

For many centuries, military strategists dreamed of a weapon that would be so powerful that it would deter any attack. Such a weapon, the atomic bomb based on nuclear fission, was discovered and used twice, in 1945. In 1950, US president Harry Truman decided to let scientists go ahead with adding the principle of fusion to that of fission and build the hydrogen bomb. The project succeeded and brought about the so-called thermonuclear revolution. Nuclear weapons turned out to be so devastating that some think they are unusable. Certain theorists, most notably Kenneth Waltz (1981), have argued that the ultimate in security would be the ultimate in deterrence, namely a situation where every unit in the states system had access to nuclear weapons. The major counterargument is simple—if nuclear weapons are so devastating that they cannot be used, then the temptation would remain for states to attempt to increase their security by arming themselves with usable weapons and capabilities. After all, the possession of nuclear weapons seems to have done little to slow down the armoring of, say, the United States, China, and Russia.

There is a key problem with seeking security by stocking up on arms, namely that others will follow suit. In a book from 1951 called *Political Realism and Political Idealism*, John Herz formulated what he called the security dilemma. On the one hand, it seems smart to spend a lot of resources on building capabilities, for it increases security. On the other hand, if the state or states you seek security against follow(s) suit, then two things happen. First, the resources you spent will be wasted, in the sense that they could have been used on something else (there will be what economists call opportunity costs), while the balance with your opponents will be the same as it was before you stocked up on new weapons. Second, and this is the rub, not only will you be worse off in the sense that you have wasted resources, you will also be worse off in the sense that the world will be a more heavily armed place than it was before you made your investment. That brings all kinds of insecurities: higher chances for accidents to happen, stronger militaries, more militarization, and so less social flexibility. This is the security dilemma: the seeking of security by building new capabilities may lead to an arms race that brings less, and not more, security. You will recall the dilemma of the stag hunt, which concerns the pros and cons of cooperating with your friends. The security dilemma concerns the pros and cons of cooperating with your enemies.

Securitization

The most important innovation in security thinking since the end of the Cold War concerns exactly how something becomes a security concern in the first place. In 1995, Danish IR scholar Ole Wæver published a chapter called "Securitization and Desecuritization" in a book called *On Security*. The chapter has become a, probably the, foundational text of the so-called Copenhagen school of security studies. Wæver's point was simple. Security is a *speech act*, with a speech act being a spoken statement that creates what it talks about—think of the baptism of a boat or the proclamation of a marriage. The wider phenomenon that the speech act is supposed to capture, and that may be brought about by other dramaturgical means as well, is performativity—the general phenomenon of something being created by being performed.[2]

A speech act is a performative utterance, so if security is a speech act, it is not the state of being without care; it is rather a state of being where one calls attention to specific phenomena and singles them out for care. In other words, something becomes a security concern once a person who is in the political position to do so lifts that phenomenon out of normal political debate and makes it a question of whether the polity can go on being itself if the potential threat in question is not addressed. Security is therefore not a fixed thing, but a process of naming certain social phenomena and having them accepted as part of an extraordinary social category called "security." It is this process of lifting a phenomenon out of everyday politics and onto the priority list of cases that is security politics, complete with its repertoire of ways to use force at a large scale, which Wæver calls *securitization*. In the 1990s, there was a debate between those who favored making phenomena such as climate change security concerns, primarily because it would heighten the attention paid to these phenomena, and those who were against this, primarily because such widening of the concept of security would mean militarizing them, because military tools are usually seen as key to answering security concerns.

Securitization reminds us that security is not only a question of building defenses and weapons piles. All that only kicks in once something has been made a threat that demands a buildup. Security is also, the Copenhagen school would say first and foremost, a question of identity, for the key question is the survival of the self of the polity in the shape that we know it. Who we are leads to what we do—identity leads to interests.[3]

So, security and identity meet in the question of how who we are leads to what we do to secure who we are. And yet, in the final analysis, on the individual level, there is no such thing as security. Sooner or later, death comes to all humans. Seeking security is but one of a number of ways of being-in-the-world. Another way altogether is to argue that dangers and challenges are good, for it alleviates our boredom by giving us something to do. Those who are in charge of polities, however, cannot think in such terms (Wolfers 1952). It is the very core of their job description to keep the polity they are leading going, and that means that it is their darned duty to worry about actual and possible dangers and challenges.

Key Questions

Should climate change be considered a security issue?

Is the structure of the states system driven by the logic of security?

Is there such a thing as security?

Notes

1. The principal text in which Rousseau ([1756] 2004) actually deals with the problem of alliances and the relations between states is in a less known discussion of a 1713 book on European peace by Charles-Irénée Castel, abbé de Saint-Pierre.

2. In the previous chapter, we discussed another instance of this, namely that the process of global governance may be the series of performances that produce the global polity.

3. Note, however, that it is also the case that what we do determines who we are, so in social science speak, we may also argue that the two phenomena are co-constitutive.

Bibliography

Abrahamsen, Rita, and Michael C. Williams. 2010. *Security beyond the State: Private Security in International Politics*. Cambridge: Cambridge University Press.

Herz, John H. 1951. *Political Realism and Political Idealism: A Study in Theories and Realities*. Chicago: University of Chicago Press.

Rousseau, Jean-Jacques. [1754] 2004. *Discourse on the Origin of Inequality*. New York: Dover.

Wæver, Ole. 1995. "Securitization and Desecuritization." In *On Security*, ed. Ronnie Lipschutz. New York: Columbia University Press.

Waltz, Kenneth. 1959. *Man, the State, and War: A Theoretical Analysis*. New York: Columbia University Press.

Waltz, Kenneth. 1981. "The Spread of Nuclear Weapons: More May Be Better." *Adelphi Papers*, no. 171. London: International Institute of Strategic Studies.

Wolfers, Arnold. 1952. "'National Security' as an Ambiguous Symbol." *Political Science Quarterly* 67 (4): 481–502.

11 ✦ International Society

The globalization of the Western states system	Period
Emerging European States System	16th and 17th centuries
European International Society	18th to mid-19th centuries
Global International Society	20th century
World Society	21st century?

Hedley Bull (1977) drew a distinction between an international or states system, on the one hand, and international society, on the other, with the difference being whether or not states share in the work of common institutions. Bull also talked about the need for states to note what other states are doing, but there can hardly be a system if states do not do that, so inter-subjectivity (to use the technical term) is surely present in both system and society. In other words, international society is system plus institutions, a system that has matured through institutionalization.

The English School

The concept of international society is a very English one (and, I must add, also a very colonial one), so much so that we often refer interchangeably to the international society approach and the English school of IR. We are talking about an approach that some trace back to an early British professor of IR, E. H. Carr. Charles Manning published his lecture series for new students at the London School of Economics under the title *The Nature of International Society*. His younger colleague Martin Wight, who we met in chapter 7, was a lifelong student of different international systems. The breakthrough for international society as a concept came when Hedley Bull published *The Anarchical Society* (1977).

The key thing for Bull was that the system may be anarchical in the sense that it has no head, that is, no overarching authority, but that does not mean that the anarchical is an unstructured realm. Bull saw five primary institutions—great powers, diplomacy, war, balance of power, and international law—as constitutive of international society. The institutions make up international society in the sense that the more *mature* the institutions—that is, the denser and more regular the interactions that make it up—the more mature the international society.

The concept of society hails from Latin *socius*, and is of course at the heart of academic social (the adjectival form of the noun society) sciences, which had been theorizing the concept for a century when Bull wrote his book. The reasons why Bull does not really touch base with this general literature on what makes society possible are, I think, two. First, his principal source of inspiration was not the social sciences, but history and, I would say principally, international law, particularly as theorized by Oxford legal scholar H. L. A. Hart. Here we have one way in which the English school is very English, in the sense that the English intellectual tradition is basically commonsensical, whereas the Continental tradition out of which the social sciences grew is more conceptual. The second reason why Bull stayed away from sociology was probably his abhorrence of what IR calls the domestic analogy, that is, treating international relations as if they were analogous to relations inside a state. To Bull, what held for a bounded state did not automatically hold for the anarchical realm between states, and it was therefore imperative to uphold this basic ontic delineation of the subject matter of IR.

Bull drew a distinction between two degrees of societal maturity. There are pluralist international societies, where members are primarily self-regarding, and solidarist international societies, where members are primarily other-regarding. In order to gauge the usefulness of this distinction, consider one institution of international society, namely international law. Up until the 1980s, there was little international humanitarian law. As a matter of fact, that concept was only coined in the 1990s. Today, there is a body of human rights law (see chapter 16). The defining precondition of this body of law is that humans have rights regardless of citizenship. Rights are seen as emanating from a human's status as a member of the species, and not from any other factor. Now, it has been argued that the existence of such law goes to show that today's international society has matured from being pluralist to the point of becoming solidarist. On the other hand, it could be argued that states differ widely in how they see the role of the state in all this. For some states, there is a tension between a state and its laws, on the one hand, and human rights, on the other. For example, in Germany, such a tension is explicitly acknowledged, and where the two bodies of law clash, international humanitarian law takes precedence. As seen from states like Germany, it is up to international society to set massive abuses of international humanitarian law straight. Other states stress that states are granting human rights, and therefore there can be no tension between state law and international humanitarian law. Indeed, it falls to the state within which human rights breaches take place to set them straight. Such tensions may usefully be discussed in terms of whether present-day international society is pluralist or solidarist. Germany's legal view is other-regarding—what happens elsewhere, say, a genocide, may be so important that international society should deal with it in unison. This is a solidarist view of international society. A state like Russia begs to differ— Russia holds that what happens inside a state, regardless of what the subject matter might be, is the business of that sovereign state, and that state should be left to deal with it. This is a pluralist view of international society. In keeping with this view, in 2015 Russia passed a law stating that rulings of the Russian Constitutional Court trump rulings of the European Court of Human Rights in The Hague. The examples demonstrate how there is a tug of war going on in contemporary international society about what the basic modus operandi should be, with states leaning toward solidarism at loggerheads with states leaning toward pluralism. Commonsensical or not, the English school hands us a pair of concepts that we may use to analyze these tensions.

There are two more basic points to be noted about the English school. First, in addition to the concept of international society, which consists of states, John Vincent, a student of Hedley Bull's, put forward the concept of world society. World society consists of a whole slew of agents, both individuals and organizations of various kinds. Where international society consists of states, world society is an attempt to capture analytically the whole slate of agents in world politics as well as the relations between them and the institutions in which they partake. The added value of the concept is to ease analysis away from focusing on maturing international society only, and so partially break with the state centrism of the English school.

Enlargement

Historically, the key precursor of today's international society was European international society. From the 18th century onward, it was enlarged by ever-new members, and now its members cover all the available planetary territory, with agreed exceptions such as the Arctic, the high seas, and the stratosphere. Note that there are still unclear boundaries. For example, there is still no delineation of where national airspace ends and space (as in, the big empty space) begins. Barry Buzan has suggested that the historical formation of today's international society through imperialism and colonialism has resulted in a composite phenomenon. There is a single-civilizational core to international society consisting of European states and European settler states, and then there are the add-ons. This is a West-and-the-rest perspective (for an alternative interpretation, see Keene 2002).

The history of international society's enlargement is certainly the history of expansion, in two principal waves. There is, first, Russia, Turkey, Siam, and the few other 18th and 19th centuries polities that were not formally colonized. Then there is the fallout from defeated empires in Europe after the First World War, principally Austria-Hungary. Finally, there is the somewhat delayed fallout from the crumbling European overseas empires after the Second World War, with decolonization bringing a number of new states into international society. There are still candidates waiting in the wings. The Palestinian Authority, Scotland, and Catalonia may serve as good examples of secessionist candidates—that is, candidate polities that are faced with a struggle with the states of which they are presently part if they want to become members of international society. The atoll polity of Tuvalu (pop. 10,500), which is now part of New Zealand, and the enormous land mass of Greenland (pop. 56,000), which is now part of Denmark, are good examples of entities that have received the go-ahead to become states both from the states that they are presently part of and from the UN, but which are for various reasons biding their time.

Any association that receives new members is faced with the challenge of socializing them, with socialization being "the process that is directed toward a state's internalization of the constitutive beliefs and practices institutionalized in its international environment" (Schimmelfennig 2000, 111–12). Every time international society receives a new member state, that member state brings with it specific ways of dealing with war, law, diplomacy, and so on. The challenge is how these specific traditions will then dovetail with the state of play of the evolving institutions of international society. For international society to function, the distance between the general way of going about, say, law, and that of any one member state's way of doing it, cannot be too great. On the other hand, international society is conceived of as an anarchical realm, so the possibilities of dictating how things should be done to any one member state are limited. Here is the general dilemma of international relations, as formulated by the English school.

Note how the English commonsensical tradition permeates the way the English school formulates its *problematique*—to many English scholars themselves, this way of formulating what IR is about seems self-evident. Not so to others. If one hails from a small state, it is not immediately obvious that great powers have a privileged managerial role in the relations between states. Serbia in the 1990s comes to mind as an example, and it is a good example, since a state made up of seven million people is seen as obviously small by everybody except itself. If one hails from a so-called revisionist state, that is, a state that thinks the international order as it stands needs a thorough overhaul, the international society approach may look like part of the problem, since it celebrates order at the cost of what a revisionist state would see as justice. An example would be India's claim to a seat on the UN Security Council: how dare a concoction of yesterday's great powers deny a seat to a one billion people plus strong state that grows out of one of the world's great civilizations and will certainly be the most populous state in the world a few years from now? Finally, a revolutionary state will by definition not have time for international society at all, since international society is propping up the regime or regimes that the revolution is directed against. A present-day example would be the movement that likes to be called the Islamic State, which sees the international order as illegitimate since it does not spring from the only real font of authority, which is Allah.

Traditions of International Thought

All these criticisms are worth pondering. Indeed, the English school has institutionalized these criticisms in a cover-all scheme of how to think about international society itself (Wight 1992). The kind of thinking that contends that there is no international society, and that institutions will not ultimately mature relations between states, is referred to by the English school as *Hobbesian*. Thinking about international society of the kind that the English school itself is promoting, which privileges relations between states as subject to social change, is referred to as *Grotian*, after the 17th-century international lawyer Hugo Grotius.[1] Revolutionary thinking of any kind (communist, religious, and so on) that would overturn international society for one reason or the other the English school refers to, perhaps a bit incongruously, as *Kantian*.[2]

The value of thinking about IR in terms of an international society lies primarily in the way it opened the discipline to historical studies and to linking what happens within specific institutions such as international law to the overall structural question of how international relations work understood as a whole. All this is particularly worthwhile as a counterweight to studies of foreign policy (see chapter 6), since a focus on international society forces the analyst to yoke the question of what one agent does to the more fundamental question of how *relations* between agents work.

Key Questions

Is international society more than the concert of great powers?

"International society is nothing but the expansion of the Western states system." Discuss.

Notes

1. As noted in chapter 7, a well-known elaboration of Martin Wight's categorization is Alexander Wendt's (1999), where "Grotian" has become "Lockian."

2. Incongruous, since Kant detailed a very specific historiosophical vision of a continuous process leading to a world state (see chapter 14), while others put in this "Kantian" category suggest all kinds of other ways of overthrowing the system.

Bibliography

Bull, Hedley. 1977. *The Anarchical Society*. London: Palgrave.

Keene, Eddie. 2002. *Beyond the Anarchical Society: Grotius, Colonialism and Order in World Politics*. Cambridge: Cambridge University Press.

Schimmelpfennig, Frank. 2000. "International Socialization in the New Europe: Rational Action in an Institutional Environment." *European Journal of International Relations* 6 (1): 109–39.

Wendt, Alexander. 1999. *Social Theory of International Politics*. Cambridge: Cambridge University Press.

Wight, Martin. 1992. *International Theory: The Three Traditions*. New York: Holmes and Meier.

12 ✦ Great Powers

> Where there is great power there is great responsibility.
>
> WINSTON CHURCHILL

In all the states systems we know of, certain states have always been seen as more powerful than others. In the Amarna system, which existed in the Bronze Age eastern Mediterranean, Egypt was the key power, and the game for the kings of the other leading powers in the system such as Hatti (the Hittite state) and Mittani was to have the pharaoh refer to them as brother instead of son. In Ancient Greece, Athens and Sparta were considered leading powers by all, and in Renaissance Italy, city-states such as Naples, Florence, Venice, and Milan were in a league of their own. In 16th and 17th century Europe, the talk was of "powers," meaning leading powers.

Modern Great Powers

During the 18th century, when treaties were drawn up, particularly but not exclusively in the wake of wars, certain powers had retained the prerogative of guaranteeing those treaties to themselves. With the exception of Spain (a state that no longer commanded the respect it once had), the European Concert that was formed after the Napoleonic Wars consisted of those states that had usually guaranteed treaties during the 18th century. In the sense that different states were held to belong to different layers whose power and hence importance varied, the European system of states was hierarchical from its very inception. It is true that there also existed a principle of sovereign equality, which worked against interventions in the internal affairs of others as well as the kind of ranking of individual states that had existed before the system took shape. This principle, however, concerned the ranking of specific states, not the ranking of layers of states.

With the coming of the new way of thinking about knowledge as something exact, and the emergence of the science of statistics, both of which developed from the inception of modernity in the mid-18th century, we also see a change in what greatness means, away from closeness to God, toward relative capabilities.

When the Congress of Vienna met in 1815 to work out a postwar order, work was done in committees. Some states—Russia, Great Britain, Austria-Hungary, Prussia, and France—partook in the work of all committees, and went on to grant themselves the sole and formal right to call envoys from one to the others ambassadors. Informally, they became the great powers (Smith 2006). Some states—Spain, Sweden, Denmark, and so on—partook in some committees and not others, and were sometimes referred to as middle powers. Those that did not partake in any committee work at all became the small powers. Note that the status of being a great power is relational—it is impossible to be great if some other units of the system are not great, but small, and so can confirm the greatness of other units by serving as a measure for comparison of certain other states' greatness.

While it is necessary for a power to be considered great to have smaller powers acknowledging it as such in practice (if not necessarily in so many words), it is not sufficient. Other great powers have to acknowledge you as one of their own, too. Great powers are like a club. Being a great power is what we often call a club good, meaning that the good does not apply to you before you are accepted into the club by extant members. Being recognized as a great power means that decision makers in other polities will take what they see as your interests into consideration when they make their own plans and reach their own decisions. This is what is meant when we say that it is constitutive of a great power that it has a *droit de regard*, or right to be considered a factor by other states. It is this right that makes a great power present at the table of other states even when absent; it exerts power in settings that its representatives do not even know exist. It exerts power simply by dint of being great. Other great powers will, at least in principle, recognize not only your existence but also what they see as your rightful interests. For this reason, rising states may aspire to great-power status, and those who possess it may try to limit the number of additional ones. For example, when Catherine the Great insisted that 18th-century Russia was a great power, she was making a claim for Russia to be included in certain specific political processes from which great powers of the day had been trying to exclude it. Since there is no way for politicians or analysts to define a great power without intervening in this essentially political process, the concept of great power has remained an essentially contested concept. The ensuing confusion surrounding the concept may be found both in historical analyses, where there are considerable yet rarely highlighted differences in usage, and in contemporary political debate.

Two Modern Usages

The expression "great power" emerged coterminously with the modern states system, and began life not as a concept, but as a (composite) word. International lawyer Emer de Vattel's definition—a power that can stand up to any combination of others—is the classic one. German historian Leopold von Ranke's ([1833] 1873) celebrated essay on the matter encapsulates the views of the German *Machtschule* (power school), and was so dominant throughout the entire 19th century that I would argue that "great power" remained a word as opposed to a concept to the very end of the century. To Ranke, as to most statesmen, great powers were states that by dint of their economic and military might were able to maintain a sphere of influence where other great powers gave them a *droit de regard*. More specifically, Kratochwil (1989, 83) identifies "the rule of a 'great power'" as "a power with system-wide interests as well as a say in matters pertaining to the management of the system. Managing the security issues in the classic conception of politics involved largely the issues of a balance of power." Although the great powers did not maintain the practice of meeting in concert for more than seven years after the 1815 Congress of Vienna, the European Concert itself survived by dint of other practices. This institutionalization of what Ranke meant by great power explains why it went largely unchallenged for so long—Ranke was simply read as summing up the received and hence obvious opinion (*doxa*) of the day.

This institutionalization also explains why, on first reading, the major theorist of power of the early 20th century and the immediate precursor of IR realists did not really add anything new on the topic of great powers. In his major work, Max Weber stated: "Nowadays one usually refers to those polities that appear to be the bearers of power prestige [*Machtprestige*] as the 'Great Powers'" (1991, 161). To Weber, prestige is not specific to the system of states, but is rather a general "irrational element" toward which every polity strives. In the states system, it is relational and means glory over other communities.

The reason why this definition does not at first appear as new is that, to Weber as to Vattel and Ranke before him, prestige is obviously tied in with military and economic factors. The comparatively superior strength and the mutually recognized spheres of influence that are constitutive of great powers may, therefore, be seen as what we would now call structural characteristics of the system of states. In the eyes of these theorists, these are characteristics of the social organization of states. Vattel and Ranke think in analytical terms, in the sense that what the agents themselves think is of no importance. It is the analyst, writing from a distance, who decides what prestige is and how it is distributed. Weber, on the other hand, is ambivalent on this issue. In some places, he writes as if the issue of prestige is analytical, whereas in others he writes as if it is what the actors themselves think about prestige that is of the essence. To Weber, prestige of culture is an intersubjective phenomenon; it is a question of how cultures assess one another. To the degree that prestige of power is tied to prestige of culture, prestige of power becomes not only an analytical question but also a question of intersubjectivity. Intersubjective meanings depend on a game of negotiation by two or more agents. Seeing a great power as intersubjectively constituted by the actors of a system is a very different thing from seeing it as structurally constituted by the system of states. Since Weber's usage was in line with the meaning commonly ascribed to the term "great power," however, this seems to have gone unnoticed at the time. A similar tension may be traced in what remains, arguably, the most widely used and explicitly realist and descriptive definition, namely that offered by Jack Levy (1983). To him, a great power is a state that plays a major role in international politics with respect to security-related issues. Accordingly, the great powers can be differentiated from other states by their military power, their interests, their behavior in general and interactions with other powers, and other powers' perception of them.

The existence of another meaning for the term "great power" became apparent only when it was spelled out in the work of the other key sociologist at Weber's time, Émile Durkheim. The context was a lecture course on the state held in 1913 but not published in its entirety until 1950. As noted in chapter 2, Durkheim saw the emergence of the modern state as emanating from a small cadre (historically, the king and his advisers). Durkheim famously describes this as an organic process, whereby the head grows an ever more finely honed system with which to operate its societal body. He maintains that this process is characteristic of the modern state from the 17th century onward. Here we have a clear-cut criterion for gauging which states are "great" and which are not. Drawing on the concept of pride, which seems close to Weber's "prestige," Durkheim (1992, 75) argues:

> As long as there are States, so there will be national pride, and nothing can be more warranted. But societies can have their pride, not in being the greatest or the wealthiest, but in being the most just, the best organized and in possessing the best moral constitution.

Durkheim's classificatory scheme is now used by statespeople about other powers. For example, during her state visit to Delhi in 2009, US Secretary of State Hillary Clinton (quoted in French 2010, xvi) stated:

> Not so long ago, the measure of a nation's greatness was the size of its military, or its economic strength, or its capacity to dominate its friends and allies. [. . .] But in this century—in the interconnected and interdependent world in which we live—greatness can be defined by the power of a nation's example.

Contemporary Usage

The two meanings of great power appear in contemporary analytical usage as well. Clear-cut examples of privileging materiality over morals may be found in Waltz (1979), who holds that the key characteristic of the existing international system is that it, similarly to the way the system of the market produces functionally similar firms, produces units that are functionally equivalent. These functionally similar units are now nation-states, and they differ in one aspect only: their power resources. Some states are greater than others, and this greatness may be explained by the characteristics of the system itself, which differentiates between its units only at this very level (see chapter 7). As William Wohlforth (1987) has argued, it follows that greatness is therefore a systemic characteristic. It has nothing to do with intersubjectivity or recognition, which should be treated as questions of foreign policy.

By contrast, a similarly clear-cut example of privileging morals may be found in Christian Reus-Smit's work, whose thrust emanates from the idea that overt institutions of IR like sovereignty are dependent on covert constitutional structures, which he defines as "coherent ensembles of intersubjective beliefs, principles, and norms that perform two functions in ordering international societies: they define what constitutes a legitimate actor, entitled to all the rights and privileges of statehood; and they define the basic parameters of rightful state action" (1999, 30).

Note, however, that both neorealists and constructivists like Reus-Smit perform ideal-typical analytics. Empirically, the two meanings may simply not lend themselves to disentanglement. The literature on what makes a power "great" suggests two ideal-typical methodologies, one of which highlights material resources, and the other civilizational standards. The only criterion for deciding which of these ideal types is the better one is fruitfulness—but there is no agreement on which is the more fruitful. We may have reached a theoretical dead end.

The clash of the two principal meanings of "great power" goes beyond the analytical realm, for the points at stake also surface in the ongoing tug-of-war between the West and the rest over who shall lead the ongoing restructuring of international relations. Both parties use both kinds of arguments. For example, moral arguments crop up when the West refers to human rights, a field within which Western states have an edge. They also crop up, however, in India's campaign to gain a permanent seat on the United Nations Security Council, where a key argument is India's alleged standing as a *moral* power, and another (and perhaps more convincing) is the moral case for giving over a billion people a voice at the key table of institutionalized international relations. Inversely, however, both President Trump's United States and the BRICS (Brazil, Russia, India, China, South Africa) make regular claims to great power status on the basis of their military or economic strength, or both.

Let me end by making what is called a reflexive point, a point about what kinds of effects our knowledge-producing practices, that is, our scientific practices, have. As seen from a great power, it is not inconsequential what scholars say and write about who is a great power and why, for such scholarly pontification may confirm or deny a state's claim to being a great power. The consequence of this is that our analyses of which states are great powers and why will be one of the factors that constitute great powers as such. Technically put, analyses of great powers are constitutive of great-power status. Our analyses are not distinct from what we study. On the contrary, our analyses feed into the phenomena we study and become a part of those phenomena. This is a general predicament for the social scientist, for social scientists study phenomena that they themselves are part of (in social science speak, this phenomenon is referred to as double hermeneutics; Giddens 1987). Knowledge practices play out within a field of power, and their results often play directly back into that field. This is what we call the power/knowledge nexus (see chapter 17). Studying social phenomena is therefore different from studying, say, astronomy. There is no way around this problem, but it should serve as a hefty reminder of the importance of the standpoints and value judgments we bring to our analyses (see chapter 1; Neumann and Neumann 2017). We also have here a reminder that the social scientist has a responsibility to at least try to think through the effects of her analyses on the phenomena she studies, to at least try to relate to the possible constitutive consequences of her own analyses of the phenomena of which social realities are made.

Key Questions

Is the UN nothing but a concert of Great Powers?

Can small powers be great in specific issue areas, and, if so, what does that tell us about international relations?

Bibliography

Durkheim, Émile. [1950] 1992. *Professional Ethics and Civic Morals*. London: Routledge.

French, Mary Mel. 2010. *United States Protocol: The Guide to Official Diplomatic Etiquette*. Lanham, MD: Rowman & Littlefield.

Giddens, Anthony. 1987. *Social Theory and Modern Sociology*. Cambridge: Polity Press.

Kratochwil, Friedrich V. 1989. *Rules, Norms, and Decisions: On the Conditions of Practical and Legal Reasoning in International Relations and Domestic Affairs*. Cambridge: Cambridge University Press.

Levy, Jack S. 1983. *War in the Modern Great Power System, 1475–1975*. Lexington: University Press of Kentucky.

Neumann, Cecilie Basberg, and Iver B. Neumann. 2017. *Situated Research Methodology—Autobiography, Field, Text*. London: Palgrave Pivot.

Reus-Smit, Christian. 1999. *The Moral Purpose of the State: Culture, Social Identity, and Institutional Rationality in International Relations*. Princeton: Princeton University Press.

Smith, Hamish M. 2006. *The Birth of a Great Power System, 1740–1815*. London: Routledge.

von Ranke, Leopold. [1833] 1973. "The Great Powers." In *The Theory and Practice of History*, ed. Georg G. Iggers and Konrad von Moltke. Indianapolis, IN: Bobbs-Merrill.

Weber, Max. 1991. *From Max Weber: Essays in Sociology*. London: Routledge.

Wohlforth, William C. 1987. "The Perception of Power: Russia in the Pre-1914 Balance." *World Politics* 39 (3): 353–81.

13 ✦ Diplomacy

Modular breakthroughs in diplomatic practice	From when
Regular contacts between culturally similar small-scale polities	5,500 years ago
Regular contacts between culturally different large-scale polities	4,000 years ago
Permanent bilateral diplomacy	15th century–
Permanent multilateral diplomacy	20th century–

Diplomacy comes from the ancient Greek *diplon*, which means to fold twice. What was folded was a document (see diploma), which served as an envoy's legitimation. The general meaning of diplomacy is the handling of relations with other polities by chosen representatives. This also extends to the social and institutional context for those relations, what those relations are, how they are performed, and with which effects. The concepts of diplomacy and diplomat were not in much use from Roman to modern times, but the three functions that are denoted by the concept— representation of a polity toward other polities; collection of information about those other polities and reporting of that information back to the home polity; negotiation with other polities on behalf of the polity one represents—are frequently found. Sometimes other functions are in play as well. The conceptual history of what we are not entirely warranted in calling "diplomacy," then, concerns variation in these three functions and how they have been conceptualized by polities and groups of polities. We are going to touch on the latter, for it is of interest that representatives of the polity of the Catholic Church in mediaeval times were called *missi*. What is really interesting, however, is how *missi* went about their functions. We find their specificity in that they did *not* fulfil the function of negotiation, but simply delivered messages. The same was the case with early modern Russian diplomats, who did not have a mandate to negotiate on behalf of the head of their polity, either. When they came to Europe and met heads of polities and their diplomats who expected to negotiate with them and found that they could not do so, there was a breakdown in communication.

With no negotiation, diplomacy did not work. The historical resolution of this impasse was that the Russian head of state learnt to delegate, and Russian diplomats learnt to negotiate. There was a change in Russian and European diplomatic culture both, and Russia entered the European institution of diplomacy.

Diplomacy is about writing texts, and it is about talk. When Winston Churchill quipped that jaw jaw is better than war war, what he meant was that it would be a good idea to try diplomacy, for it just might avert going to war. Note, however, that the widely held view that diplomacy is the opposite of war does not hold true. The two shade into one another, for diplomatic tools include everything up to and including threats of war. When such a threat is used as a diplomatic tool, we are talking about gunboat diplomacy. Furthermore, diplomacy continues in parallel to war. War does not mean that diplomacy ceases, although it does mean that formal diplomatic contacts are broken off. Informal contacts continue, in the form of back channels and third-party representation. Back channels are indirect and nonpublicized ways in which polities communicate. Third-party communication means that some other polity is representing the polity that has broken off formal relations with the host polity. For example, when the United States broke off diplomatic relations with revolutionary Cuba and withdrew its representation to that state (1961–2015), the Swiss embassy to Havana simply opened a new desk that handled American diplomatic concerns on Washington's behalf.

Note that this also demonstrates how the United States, which has a tradition of not talking to the enemy, was nonetheless willing to do so out of the public eye. Diplomacy frequently displays this kind of duality, where diplomats signal to their home audience and also third audiences that they are standing firm, not taking notice of the other, not talking to terrorists, and so forth, whereas in actual fact, contacts are simply on a back-channel basis. By this token, lists that proscribe contacts with certain polities, for example, terrorist lists, should rarely be taken to mean that there is no contact whatsoever. The best argument for continuing to talk is that, when one eventually vanquishes or is vanquished by another polity, one will have to talk to that polity anyway, so why not start right away?

The concept of diplomacy is often reserved for relations between states only. From a social science perspective, this is unwarranted, for doing so privileges relations within states systems and occludes other relations. This is problematic politically, but also analytically, for it reads out a number of relations between polities that we need to analyze in order to get as full an understanding of global politics as possible. On the other hand, we cannot use diplomacy as a catchall for all contacts that take place between polities. In order to be diplomatic interaction, at least one of the parties to it must be a formal or informal representative of a polity. For example, if a trade ministry delegates a businessman to undertake a fact-finding mission, we are warranted in categorizing this as a case of trade diplomacy. Historically, such specific interactions were important, and typically involved nonspecialized personnel (that is, people who had no specific knowledge of or training in diplomacy) who were already in the polity with which interaction was needed, or had knowledge of it from previous interactions, say as traders, travelers, or missionaries. When we are talking about nonhyphenated diplomacy, however, we are talking about interactions where at least one of the parties also takes a more general view of the relation, as when one sends, say, a sports team to another country with a view not only to play matches but also to open up a more general slate of relations.

Ancient Diplomacy

If we think of diplomacy as institutionalized interaction between polities, early examples would include hunters and gatherers, who often arranged free passage to material resources and ritually important stuff like the building of and gathering around ancient monuments, as, for example, Stonehenge. The first documented diplomatic *system*, however, we find in Anatolia and around the eastern Mediterranean in the middle of the second millennium before our era (Neumann 2012). Around 1334–1336 BCE, the revolutionary Egyptian pharaoh Akhenaten built a new capital. When it was excavated in the late 19th century close to the village of Tell el-Amarna, from which the system takes its name, archaeologists found a whole library of stone tablets. Some of these contained correspondence with other rulers, and it is primarily from these sources that we know how the system worked.

Most of the correspondence was on trade, but there were also peace agreements. If we look for elements that may tell us something about the basic political form of this system, we find that the language used was Akkadian. This is important, for it was not the language of any one of the member polities, but had been the official language of a by then defunct empire. The two elements that stand out, however, are religion and kinship. Religion and the taking into consideration of the other parties' gods is taken very seriously, to the extent that one peace treaty explicitly states that peace is made not only between the respective kings but also between the respective gods. Kinship exerts itself in patterns of intermarriage between royal houses, but also in wider discourse. As noted in chapter 7, Egypt was the hegemon of this system, and all the subordinate polities kept up a steady campaign for recognition on a par with Egypt. This took the form of trying to get the pharaoh to call you brother instead of son. In other words, the relations of the system were thought of in kinship terms.

We find the same phenomenon among all known early (in the sense of not highly differentiated) polities. For example, when the United States of America was founded and its political principles were to be conveyed to Native Americans, the way to do this was to draw on kinship terms and say things like Uncle Sam has two sons, New York and Connecticut. One particularly imaginative use of kinship in diplomacy we find in ancient Greece, where Greeks would "discover" that some polity, typically a barbarian one that was growing too strong to be ignored, say the Macedonians, were "actually" kin. What we see here is that kinship is used as what anthropologists call a myth, by which is meant not just a fiction, but a fiction that fills the important purpose of being a general matrix for thinking about more specific stuff. For diplomacy, kinship is such a myth, for it sets the scene for representation, information gathering, and negotiation to commence. The key to ancient diplomacy, as for diplomacy in general, is recognition. At a minimum, a polity wants to be recognized as such, and, at a maximum, it wants to be recognized as a polity with certain qualities.

Sublime Diplomacy and Gift Exchange

Rome saw itself as the epitome of splendor. It was quick to recognize other polities as long as they had a king, and if they did not have a king, Rome would make certain to name one. A key practice of Roman diplomacy was to "host" one or more members of barbarian polities in Rome as honored guests who also served as hostages. In this way, when succession struggles arose, Rome would have a suitably Romanized candidate for the barbarian throne at hand. Rome was also in the habit of dishing out sundry resources to barbarians to keep them reasonably quiet, but also to facilitate their Romanization. Barbarians responded by shaping their courts on the Roman model. When Rome fell, barbarians perpetuated a number of Roman practices. In this way Roman diplomacy and other Roman institutions, not least Roman law, survived in hybridized forms in what was becoming mediaeval Europe.

Byzantium, the eastern part of the Roman Empire that lasted until 1453, perfected these policies, and particularly the art of knocking foreign visiting dignitaries to Constantinople out by the display of sheer splendor. The expression "Byzantine diplomacy" is still used about such displays. The basic idea was to stimulate all the senses of the visitors: a rising throne for the eyes, roaring mechanical lions and fluttering birds for the ears, fine incense for the nose, diaphanous silks for the fingertips, and rich food and drink for the palate. The intended effect was to impress on foreign envoys the sublimity of the emperor and the empire. All humans require food and drink at regular intervals, and all humans have an appreciation of "the beautiful" as a form, although the substance of what exactly is considered beautiful varies widely. In mediaeval East Asia, we also find display. Here it tended to center on troupes of artists and jugglers. The Byzantines were simply particularly good at two general human practices—eating together and dazzling people—that we find in all diplomatic repertoires.

We find religion, kinship, a quest for recognition, and display wherever there is diplomacy. One important reason why we may see shades of the transhistorical here is that all these elements are also on display in the system of Iroquois diplomacy, which seems to have been operative from the mid-fourteenth century onward. This is long before European colonists arrived, so we can be absolutely certain that Iroquois diplomacy emerged independently of other known diplomatic systems. To find that similar practices anchor Iroquois diplomacy as anchor other known diplomatic systems is therefore a strong indication that we have necessary and, if we add one more practice, even sufficient elements of a diplomatic system.

The element to add is gift exchange. Again, exactly what is given varies widely, but it is always something. Historically, East Asian diplomacy was particularly big on gift exchange, so much so that references are often made to a "tribute system" centering on China. You should keep in mind, however, that the terms of tribute varied widely historically, and that what China gave in exchange was often more valuable than what it received.

Furthermore, diplomatic gifts offered as what the Chinese preferred to see as tribute were sometimes immaterial. Sacred music would be one example of this.

That gift exchange is central to diplomacy is not surprising given that gift giving, receiving, and reciprocity may be seen as constitutive of socially binding ties. There is no such thing as a free gift. A gift always comes with an expectation of a countergift, and so the gift cycle keeps us committed to one other (Mauss [1925] 1990).

Permanent Diplomacy

In 1455, the duke of Milan sent a certain Nicodema de Pontremoli to Genoa in order to set up a permanent diplomatic representation. Within a few decades, permanent representation was in evidence in other Italian city-states as well. The rule up until then had been that diplomacy happened either by way of embassies—trips undertaken by a representative of some ruler to some other ruler that could sometimes last for years but were always one-offs—or congresses—congregations of representatives of polities, typically religious. This was something new: an entire system of representatives of sending polities that stayed put in host countries. "Embassy" changed meaning, and became the building where the permanent representative executed his business (and sometimes lived; an ambassador's domicile is called his residence and may or may not be colocated with the embassy he or she heads). The system spread, first to France, then during the 17th century to all parts of Europe, and then to the rest of the world.

When permanent diplomacy appeared, there was already a consulate institution in place in the eastern Mediterranean. It also spread west and north, first to the Baltic Sea, and then to the ports and inland cities in between. From the end of the 18th century onward, state differentiation in Europe had reached a level where ministries that were specifically engaging with foreign affairs appeared (see chapter 6). During the 20th century, these three distinct institutions—the diplomatic service, the consular service, and the foreign ministry—were merged by states into a unified service, first in Sweden in 1906, and then around the world.

In the wake of the Second World War, the number of diplomatic missions (embassies to state capitals, general consulates headed by a consul with ambassadorial rank to cities that are held to be important by the sending state, delegations to international organizations) has exploded, as has the number of state and IO diplomats. At the beginning of the 20th century, they numbered in the thousands. At the beginning of the 21st century, they numbered in the hundreds of thousands. It is sometimes argued that diplomacy is on the wane. It only takes a short historical summing up to demonstrate that, in institutional terms, diplomacy is a roaring success story.

The same can be said about diplomatic conferences. There was a time when these were far and few between: Augsburg 1555, Westphalia 1648, Vienna 1815, Berlin 1878. Then things sped up. Huge conferences may now only be once a decade or so apart (Cairo 1994 on population and development, Copenhagen 2009 on climate change), and in addition there are all kinds of minor meetings to take into consideration.

Diplomats take a keen interest in the study of technical aspects of international relations—how to organize diplomatic services most effectively, how to use cultural knowledge of the host country to maximum effect, and so on. Diplomats specialize in taking the world as they find it and then try to get the stuff at hand done, be that to represent one's polity at a society dinner, close a trade deal, visit a national in prison, plan an art exhibition, or write a report about a local event. Diplomats are the ones who really work in the engine room of international relations (Sending, Pouliot, and Neumann 2015). As with so many success stories, there is no dearth of people who mimic diplomatic practices. Military attachés, foreign news correspondents, and development workers are but three of the groups that shape their expatriate ("expat") communities along the lines spearheaded by diplomats.

Diplomats have also proven adept at roping in new specialists to deal with new tasks. The most striking example of this is perhaps so-called public diplomacy—diplomatic work geared toward changing the policy of another polity by changing the attitudes and opinions of that polity's population. Public diplomacy was a favorite preserve of early revolutionary regimes—American, French, Russian—that wanted to spread the word. In the interwar period, it became a staple of European diplomacy in general, and is now a global practice.

IR scholars were slow to study diplomacy as an institution. For decades, they rather concentrated on how diplomats participated in the decision-making process that is foreign policy making, and left studies of diplomatic practices to practitioners. The breakthrough for theory came in 1987, when American IR scholar James Der Derian brought the concept of alienation to the study of diplomacy and published a book where he defined diplomacy as the mediation of estrangement.

To sum up, diplomacy is about representing a polity in and to other polities, gathering information and reporting on what happens in other polities, and negotiating with other polities on behalf of the polity one represents. With globalization, we have a whole slate of agents—journalists, academics, party planners, spies, sundry experts in trans- and subnational politics, and the list goes on—that specialize in some of the practices that make up diplomacy. Diplomacy and diplomats continue to thrive, however, for only they work relations between polities with a view to managing *all* of these aspects.

Key Questions

Should the concept of diplomacy be reserved for state interaction?

In which ways is contemporary diplomacy Euro-centric?

Bibliography

Der Derian, James. 1987. *On Diplomacy: A Genealogy of Western Estrangement*. Oxford: Blackwell.

Mauss, Marcel. [1925] 1990. *The Gift: The Form and Reason for Exchange in Archaic Societies*. London: Norton.

Neumann, Iver B. 2012. *At Home with the Diplomats: Inside a European Foreign Ministry*. Ithaca: Cornell University Press.

Sending, Ole Jacob, Vincent Pouliot, and Iver B. Neumann. 2015. *Diplomacy and the Making of World Policy*. Cambridge: Cambridge University Press.

14 ✦ War and Peace

> [W]ar is not merely an act of policy but a true political instrument, a
> continuation of political intercourse carried on with other means.
>
> CARL VON CLAUSEWITZ

Some 5,500 years ago, Indo-Europeans invented the wagon, which made it
possible to bring the provisions needed to spend a prolonged period of time
in the Eurasian steppe, and some 1,500 years later, the horse-driven, spoke-
wheeled chariot emerged. Indo-Europeans trekked into Anatolia and the
Fertile Crescent, probably as mercenaries, and took over earlier polities
there with their superior warfare technology. Some centuries later, ragged
bands of armed foot soldiers threw themselves against the well-established
polities of the eastern Mediterranean. Swords and shields protected these
soldiers from chariots, and, helped by a little ice age, Egypt and the other
great powers of the Amarna system were brought down around 1200 BCE.
This was in effect the end of the Mediterranean Bronze Age.

With the emergence of Greek city-states in the 9th century BCE, war
was in the hands of the hoplites, that is, the free soil-working men of Greek
city-states on standing military duty. At fairly regular intervals, there would
be agreed hoplite wars, where the armies of two cities pushed against one
another, sword in hand, until one party was pushed back and weakened
by losses to such a degree that the survivors fled the scene. The victors
proceeded to hang part of the captured armor in trees to celebrate. At the
more gruesome scenes of battle, women and children would be taken into
captivity and put to work or sold as slaves.

This is what has been called the Western way of war: a consecutive
series of battles that follow established procedures and ideally come to a
head in a final battle.[1] The object is to break the other party's will and get
one's way. From Thucydides via Hobbes and, I think, to this day, there are
three groups of causes for war: fear (of attack), glory (honor and status

enhancement), and material gain (territory, people, resources). If violence is perpetrated in other ways, for example by insurgency, unexpected and sudden terrorist attacks on civilian targets, or sabotage, we are, as my use of concepts other than war just now was meant to capture, loath to call it war.

Indo-Europeans are not alone in their focus on battles. In what we now call the Americas, battles were known as one form of large-scale violence. The Aztecs were particularly trusting of the practice of battles in subduing surrounding populations. Note, however, that when foreign soldiers were captured, they would sit quietly and wait for their ritual execution (and, quite often, subsequent consumption). Running away was not part of the game. Why not? Well, that's a moot question; that was just the way things were done around there. As you will see from this example, the Western way of war is a culturally distinct phenomenon. It is a bundle of evolving practices, an institution. As people kill one another, they also confirm war as an institution. Greeks and Romans had rules for how and why to go to war (*ius ad bellum*) and what you could and could not do in war (*ius in bello*). With the emergence of international society, war became the object of ever more lawmaking. Rules and laws are broken, but the fact that rules are not always followed does not necessarily mean that the institutions that they uphold disappear. A *casus belli*—reason for going to war—was usually given, as was notice of an attack. When imperial Japan attacked Pearl Harbor without giving fair warning in 1941, this was certainly not the first surprise attack in world history. The United States was nonetheless outraged.

In 1928, Western states made what turned out to be a misguided attempt at ending war by legal means. Following initiatives from the French and US foreign ministers Aristide Briand and Frank Kellogg, war was outlawed completely, which in international society terms is to say that politicians tried to subsume the institution of war under the institution of law. I think we are warranted in saying that this did not prove a political success. The letter of the law came up a bit short. Nonetheless, when the victors initiated their tribunals at Nuremburg and Tokyo after the Second World War, the Kellogg-Briand Pact was the basis for the proceedings and, to this day, the UN Charter's §4(2) states that war is unlawful.

If war is an institution, it is intersubjective, that is, the result of human interaction. This means that war is a changing phenomenon. One way of thinking about it is to give that change a direction, as does, for example, German-English sociologist Norbert Elias, who postulates that history should be read as a civilization process. He argues that, historically, war becomes more rule-based. It is also sublimated into sports. When a sport like American football looks so much like war, an Eliasian reading is to argue that, at some point in the civilization process, conflict between communities was stylized and ritualized as sports matches of a particular kind rather than as blood-drawing battles with sharp weapons.

Four Questions about War

The changing face of war may also be studied less teleologically, by asking four questions of any one period, place, or war: Who? With what? In which way? For what?

(1) Who, that is, which polities, are the warring parties? According to current international law, only states may wage war. This means that combatants other than state soldiers have a precarious position. Everything that concerns the use of force between entities that are not states may be called something else than war—insurgency, for example. Personnel that are not in state uniform will not have the full rights of captured enemies as spelled out in the Geneva Conventions (1929–49) on humanitarian treatment in war and may end up, say, interned by the United States in Guantanamo Bay, Cuba, for more than a decade and made the subject of torture. Who the warring parties are seen to be, and who they actually are, matters a lot to the character of war. Note also the question of personnel; there is by now a large gender literature on war, with one point being that males between 18 and 35, the very same group that is cross-culturally over-represented in crime statistics (where these are to be found), are also the mainstay of armies. Jean Bethke Elshtain (1987) talks about males as the violent many and the pacific few, with women then being the pacific many and violent few.

(2) With what is the fight being fought? We already touched on how technology constantly reconfigures the face of war. There is an interesting literature on nuclear weapons. As noted in chapter 10, many think that they cannot be used, and some think that a world where as many states as possible have nuclear weapons is the ultimate in peace, for the possibility of nuclear war deters states from attacking. Others worry about the possible use of so-called tactical nukes, that is, nukes used on the battlefield. And then

there is what used to be referred to as a revolution in military affairs—what is the importance of warfare taking place at night, with infrared equipment, or from afar, with drones?

(3) In which way is war being fought? Talk about revolutions in military affairs was also fueled by changes in this respect. We talk about micro planning and deployment of specific war practices as tactics, and about macro planning about how to secure, coordinate, and deploy resources for purposes of warfare as strategy. Planning for the battle is tactics, planning for the war is strategy. In between is what is called the operational level. One example of how important this is may be seen in how the Mongol-led steppe forces took over most of the known world from the mid-1200s onward. It was not only that Chinggis Khan's forces had superior equipment (first and foremost the composite bow, which packed a lot of power and could be used in all directions from horseback), but also that they were the only forces of the day to think in terms of strategy. Chinggis and his successors also had another advantage. Since every able-bodied male was by definition a soldier, there were no civil-military relations among the Mongols. The point is sometimes made that Europeans—Swedes during the Thirty Years' War (1618–1648), Frenchmen during the French Revolution—were the first to raise mass armies. This is clearly wrong. By then, every able-bodied male on the Eurasian steppe had been a mounted soldier for millennia.

Here we have a nice reminder of why it pays analytically to ask the question posed by Samuel Finer (1988): Why is not the man on horseback in control everywhere? The answer is the coming of agricultural and then industrial society, which is too complex to be run efficiently by military leadership. Civil-military relations are usually fraught with conflict, for politicians want different kinds of things, whereas well-trained soldiers simply want to achieve a specific target. From the point of view of the military, politicians tend to be easily diverted and corrupt. For example, when the northern barbarians (Xiongnu) had repeatedly conquered the Han during the centuries before our era, the Chinese military repeatedly pointed out that the answer was to beat them at their own game and develop a Chinese cavalry. The politicians, who had a material stake in maintaining foot soldiers, kept on refusing. From the point of view of politicians, though, the military grunts hardly have it in them to lift their head from above their guns. They only see the immediate task and the enemy in front of them, not the whole picture.

(4) For what is the war fought? Is it for survival of the polity? That could be the case when armored Greek citizens (hoplites) lined up in a field and engaged one another in close combat. In extreme cases (as Thucydides describes the fate of Melos in *The History of the Peloponnesian War*), the surviving males were killed and the women and children taken or sold as slaves. Maori warfare also tended to be existential. During one of the main sea battles of the First World War, the Battle of Jutland, the British admiral, Sir John Jellicoe, thought that he could lose the war in an afternoon, while less was at stake for his German counterpart. That made for different tactics on the part of the two admirals. Warring parties will try to take warfare to one another's soil, but the downside of that is, as the United States has experienced in places like Vietnam, Iraq, and Afghanistan, that soldiers and populations that fight on their home soil for survival of their polity tend to fight much harder than do those fighting abroad. It is harder to break their will, and that is the entire point of warfare. If war is the continuation of politics by other means (Clausewitz), then we may also think of motivations for war with Hobbes (who took his clue from Thucydides, whose *History* he translated into English), who thought that fear, glory, and gain were the three reasons for waging it.[2]

Peace

There are a number of reasons why war has been studied intensely, whereas peace has hardly been studied at all. One is that peace, despite its various conceptual configurations, is often defined simply as a negative default, as the absence of war (Richmond and Berenskoetter 2016). Such a definition is specious, for scientific reasons—it is not optimal to define a phenomenon by dint of a lack—and also for empirical reasons, for it implies that war is the rule and peace the exception, whereas world historically, it is the other way around. As do all concepts, peace has its history. As pointed out by Belgian IR scholar Jorg Kustermans (forthcoming), in the European Middle Ages, peace was understood as a graded phenomenon, with heavenly peace (Pax Jerusalem) anchoring earthly social peace, which was a question of being carefree and at ease but also of caring for one's fellow humans. Social peace then anchored political peace. Peace treaties between rulers were sealed with a kiss, which was also the key symbol of peace.

With the rise of the states system, the weakening of the Catholic Church, and the memories of the Wars of Religion, peace came to be re-defined to denote the need to hold back and distance one's state from the affairs of other states. For a state to live in peace meant that it policed its social life against incursions from the outside and considered what happened on the outside with a certain indifference. Peace treaties became more technical affairs. Kustermans then argues that this kind of "modern peace" is now coming to an end, its place taken by democratic peace. Democratic peace, he argues, is in certain ways a return to a mediaeval way of thinking about peace, in that it involved the people (Gr. *demos*) directly; it is involved and combative rather than stand-offish and indifferent as was modern peace.

Democratic Peace

Conflict studies have evolved some approaches to sustainable peace where the focus is on building trust on the individual level, be that among leaders or in communities. However, the dominating approach to peace over the last decades has been a macro approach, the so-called democratic peace.

In 1983, Yale IR scholar Michael Doyle published two articles in the journal *Philosophy and Public Affairs*. The second article was explicitly political in spelling out what liberal democracies should do to build peace (it was, basically, the exact opposite of what then US president, and conservative crusader, Ronald Reagan did). We, however, are interested in the first article, which argued that liberal democracies do not fight one another.

The argument started from the observation that liberal democracies tend not to go to war with one another. Note that they are not more peaceful than other states—this is what is referred to as the discredited monistic thesis (Lat. *mono*, one: one state only is the object of theorizing)—for they wage war just as much if not more than other states. They are only peaceful to one another—this is the dualistic thesis. Might this be because it is so much easier to signal intentions to the other party when regimes are similar, so that escalation of conflicts to the level of war is avoided? No, democracies are as bad at signaling as is everyone else, and also between themselves. Is this simply because they are similar? No, for communist states, which also share a regime type, have a record of waging war on one another. May it be because, in the history of liberal democracies, there has always been a liberal hegemon, that is, a first among equals—Britain before the Second World War, the United States afterward—that has kept the other democracies in line, by hook and by crook? A factor, but not enough, Doyle argues.

Doyle thinks the German philosopher Immanuel Kant (1991) hatched the basic explanation already in 1790, in his recipe for eternal peace.[3] Kant argued that even societies populated by devils, as he put it, would be able to keep the peace if only three preconditions were fulfilled. First, states had to be republican, by which Kant meant that citizens would carry the costs of going to war (whereas autocrats will not, but will pass on the dying and the other costs to their subjects). Second, some kind of pacific union, that is, some kind of institutional arrangement or "pact," would have to be entered into. Third, each and every state had to extend hospitality to every comer. Evolution would do the rest, for as people interacted by trading and other forms of reciprocity, they would have to evolve ways of living together. Humans are, as it were, asocially social. Kant didn't care that this did not look like a viable practical plan at the time, for he held that what is possible in theory must also be possible in practice.

Doyle's argument is the epitome of liberal IR. He is against the realist reading of the international, which stresses how war will simply break out because of human nature (fear, striving for glory, and gain; Hobbes) or because there is nothing there to stop it (as argued by Kenneth Waltz in *Man, The State, and War* [1959]). After the end of the Cold War, Doyle's articles became a key inspiration for an entire academic cottage industry known as the "democratic peace" (DP).[4]

DP theory concentrates on three basic points. First, it discusses to what degree the preconditions mentioned by Kant and Doyle are sufficient, if something is missing, and to what degree the alternative explanations mentioned by Doyle (signaling/technology, similarity of regime types, trade guaranteed by a hegemon) are valid. It is striking how little DP has added to Doyle's *problematique* in the last three and a half decades. Second, DP discusses areas of validity (fine-graining democracy, how mature democracies have to be, and so forth), also an agenda drawn up by Doyle. Third, DP works on the levels of theoretical argument and statistical correlations, as did Doyle. Where theoretical argument has scarcely become more sophisticated since Doyle published his articles in 1983, the correlational analyses definitely have.

No conclusion to the argument about the possibility of the absence of war is in sight. We know that, in what is now the southwest corner of the United States, people seem to have lived in peace in the 10,000 years leading up to the Common Era (in the periods that archaeologists refer to as Clovis), only to stop doing so when population density increased at the beginning of the 1st century CE. This demonstrates that prolonged peace among humans is possible, but such an insight does not necessarily tell us much about today's world, where population is dense all over the livable globe. So, let me end by pointing to an alternative reading of the entire question regarding the use of force, as formulated by French philosopher Michel Foucault: every age inscribes violence in its own way.

Key Questions

Do wars really happen because there is nothing to prevent them?

Are democracies peace loving?

Notes

1. Contrast this to the so-called Eastern way of war as found in Sun Tzu's *The Art of War* ([5th century BC] 1963), where a greater emphasis is placed on intelligence, ruses, and psychological domination of the enemy over direct confrontation in battle.

2. The classical formulation of Western warfare is Carl von Clausewitz's *On War* (written between 1816 and 1830; 1976). A Prussian general, Clausewitz wrote it in the aftermath of the Napoleonic Wars to account for the successes of Napoleon on the battlefield.

3. For a discussion of Kant's writings and their reception in IR, see Hurrell 1990.

4. The other key source was J. David Singer's Correlates of War project, begun in 1963, a concerned project aiming to build knowledge that could help forestall a nuclear war.

Bibliography

Clausewitz, Carl von. 1976. *On War*. Princeton: Princeton University Press.
Doyle, Michael W. 1983a. "Kant, Liberal Legacies, and Foreign Affairs, Part 1." *Philosophy and Public Affairs* 12 (3): 205–35.
Doyle, Michael W. 1983b. "Kant, Liberal Legacies, and Foreign Affairs, Part 2." *Philosophy and Public Affairs* 12 (4): 323–53.
Elshtain, Jean Bethke. 1987. *Woman and War*. Chicago: University of Chicago Press.
Finer, Samuel E. 1988. *The Man on Horseback: The Role of the Military in Politics*. Boulder, CO: Westview Press.

Hurrell, Andrew. 1990. "Kant and the Kantian Paradigm in International Relations." *Review of International Studies* 16 (3): 183–205.

Kant, Immanuel. [1790] 1991. "Perpetual Peace: A Philosophical Sketch." In *Kant: Political Writings*. Cambridge: Cambridge University Press.

Kustermans, Jorg. Forthcoming. *The Cultural Practice of Democratic Peace: Intimate, Sacred, Combative*.

Richmond, Oliver P., and Felix Berenskoetter. 2016. "Peace." In *Concepts in World Politics*, ed. Felix Berenskoetter. London: Sage.

Sun Tzu. 1963. *The Art of War*. Oxford: Oxford University Press.

Waltz, Kenneth. 1959. *Man, the State, and War: A Theoretical Analysis*. New York: Columbia University Press.

15 ✦ Balance of Power

European states balancing against	Period
Universal monarchy	Latter 17th century
Hegemony	18th and 19th centuries
State interests	19th and 20th centuries
Quantitative jump to global level	21st century

One sometimes wonders if the "power" in "the balance of power" is power understood as polity—as in small and great powers (see chapter 12)—or if it is power as the ability to make others do what they otherwise would not have done, which is the minimum definition of power. Of course, the two are related—great powers are great because they can make things happen. It is, nonetheless, important to avoid confusion on this key point. Historically, "the balance of power" was sometimes used in the meaning of the European states system, that is, a "balance of powers," with powers being states. This is what students of rhetoric call *pars pro toto*—denoting the whole by evoking one of its parts—for the balance of power is indeed one of the institutions of the European states system. The balance of power is not synonymous with the European states system or international society. That much is clear.

Power goes back to Latin *potestas*, a root that also gave us potency. It has to do with the ability to make things happen. Balance of power belongs in a setting where there is no dominating overarching authority, so that different polities may feel one another out. As established by Morten Andersen (2016), while the idea of balance between polities is older, the concept of balance of power crops up toward the end of the Thirty Years' War (1618–48), that is, in the context of the consolidation of the European states system. You will recall that, at this time, first Italian city-states and then European international society had torn themselves away from the idea that Christendom was the only important polity in this world. The mediaeval ideal of the universal monarchy was not only on the wane, it was also about to go from being an ideal to being abhorred by the emerging polities. Each and every polity was striving toward more room for maneuver, more lee-way, and the big no-no was that one polity should emerge as a hegemon, that is, a first among equals that could dominate the others. In its basic form, the balance of power was the ideal of nonhegemony, a celebration of what we now call technical anarchy, with anarchy being a situation with no ruler. If the balance were kept, universal monarchy would not materialize, and there would be peace. The balance of power was, therefore, held to be a good thing, for it was in the public interest.

In a religious sense, a balance may be God-given or natural, but, in the early European states system, there was a movement away from the God-given and the naturally guaranteed and toward the human-made. The bal-ance of power was understood as constructed, as a consciously maintained phenomenon. If something is to be kept in balance, that something has to be fairly constant. It is, therefore, no coincidence that the balance of power emerged together with the concept of interest. You may think that inter-ests are transhistorical, but in the context of the European states system, that would be a mistake. Understood as a concept, "interest" as we use it is a modern phenomenon, and giving it pride of place in political life is very modern indeed. The entire ancient Greek tradition, and indeed most other cultures, focused on honor as the key goal of life, for individuals, but also for poleis. Plato and Thucydides were among those who insisted most strongly that the pursuit of honor, which they saw as natural and good, should not be allowed to be all-consuming, for then reason would simply be shunted aside. This *problematique* was alive and well among the mediaeval European aristocracy, and survived into the 17th century. In-deed, at that time, passions were the key concept of politics. In order to check the passions of one state, other states had to muster counterpassions. These counterpassions were called interests, and it was with this meaning that the concept of "interest" entered political life. Albert O. Hirschman (1997) has written a highly instructive book about the shift from thinking about politics primarily in terms of passions (which have to do with honor), toward thinking about them in terms of interests (which have to do with reason). This shift is tied up with a key change in how European politics were classed (see chapter 19). The aristocracy, which specialized in the use of armed force, lived their lives according to a code of honor. Honor may be defined as the right to respect. If an individual or a group does not get the respect it feels entitled to, the obvious answer is to *demand* that respect, and to fight for it. Such an ethos, variants of which may still be found in a number of locations throughout the world, puts a premium on passions. The emerging bourgeoisie was different from all that. They lived by an ethos of trade and knowledge, not honor. That spells an interest-based existence. As class hegemony shifted from the aristocracy to the bourgeoisie, so the focus of European politics shifted from passions to interests.

This shift has interesting affinities with the relationship between realist and liberal readings of international relations. Up until the beginning of the 20th century, realism was associated with the passions, and liberalism with the interests. When liberals argued in favor of common interests—common interest in trade, common interest in keeping the peace, common interest in building up a body of law and international organizations—the standard realist answer was that this would not succeed, for the passions would get the better of statesmen, and no cooperation would ensue. It was only after the Second World War that realists became big on "the national interest." So, the balance of power is intimately intertwined with the emergence of interests as a new focus of politics. It is indeed so intertwined that we must conclude that what we now think of as the balance of power has liberal roots (Boucoyannis 2007). I stress this because so many IR scholars are ahistorical about realism and interests. They argue as if realists have this age-old focus on interests. That is simply not the case, and we should not forget it. Traditionally, the focus of realism was on passion, honor, and status, not on interests.

Empirically, in the 17th and 18th century the balance of power was used as an argument by a number of states against states that were on their way to becoming hegemonic—Spain, the Netherlands, Austria, then France (Burke [1790] 1982). Balance of power talk was particularly popular in Britain, and there was a reason for that: as an offshore presence, the idea emerged that it was somehow "natural" that Britain was the balancer of the system. Balance of power talk became a particular resource for Britain. One could quip that Britain got the power, and the Continent got the balance.

In the 1750s, the very idea of a balance of power, which had by then become a commonplace, was attacked by German lawyers as being abstract nonsense. The proponents of science—specific knowledge that could be established by reference to practices—became increasingly wary of sweeping historical generalizations such as the balance of power. These new scientists looked at the historical record and the attempts at measuring the balance of power and saw failure. The debate between proponents and detractors of the balance of power has been with us ever since.

Balance of power then goes through a metamorphosis of modernity, which has to do with the shift from focusing on passions to focusing on interests. In a world of passions, the balance of power is a counterweight to universal monarchy and hegemony—it is an honor-saving mechanism for all those agents that are not the one seeking hegemony. Balance of power is therefore in the public interest. In a world of *raison d'état*, that is, a world of state interests as opposed to a general public interest, on the other hand, the balance of power is *not* the alternative to the public interest, for the idea of interest is changing its abode. Public interest—the interest of all—is becoming less important, and the interest of states is becoming more important. The balance of power becomes a way of talking not about the public interest, but of celebrating the coexistence of the interests of various states. The proponents of the balance of power were able to consecrate it as part of international law, and it remained so until the end of the 19th century.

Trust in Numbers

Proponents of the balance of power also benefited from the 19th century passion for *measuring* the balance of power. The idea that things would be more real if they were measured was not new. As Theodore Porter demonstrates in his book *Trust in Numbers* (1996), it reaches back to the 13th century. It was, however, only as modernity became embedded that states began to take one another's measure in a literal sense. The preferred measures were coal and steel output, for these were at the heart of industrial output. One particularly popular proxy—that is, something one measures in order to measure something else—was the length of railway tracks. Coal was needed to fire the furnaces that produced steel, and steel was needed to build railway tracks. So, the thinking went, if one measured railway tracks, then one also measured coal and steel production (the logical flaw here is of course that different states will spend different fractions of their steel output on railways). Another reason why railways became the proxy was the importance of railways for troop transport—railways had some direct bearing on military maneuverability.

Once states started to measure one another, certain military strategists thought they had found an objective measure for power. A proper measurement for power, so the argument went, could mean that power would become to politics what money is to economics, namely a universal equalizer. The margin for error in assessing the relative strength of states would fall away, or at least be greatly reduced. This hope turned out to be misplaced. Power simply does not work that way. There are two basic reasons for this. First, there is something intangible about power resources. Consider American IR scholar John Mearsheimer's (2014, 57) definition of power as "specific assets or material resources that are available to a state." It is hard to know which material resources one should use as a proxy for measuring power. I have mentioned railways. Other key historical candidates have included the size of fighting forces, the largest classes of ships, and nuclear arsenals. It is even harder to pin down "specific assets." These obviously include good strategy, good logistics, and good leadership, but what about things like fighting morale and support for the war among the population? One theoretical concept that is very important here was hatched by Arab historian Ibn Khaldoun in 1377 (2015). The Arabic term for it is *asabiyyah* and it means something like cohesion of the polity. The greater the *asabiyyah*, the greater the action capacity. IR scholars have tried to theorize this aspect of politics under the rubric of "identity." As noted in the previous chapter, if you bring war to a polity's core area, *asabiyyah* will increase, for the polity will galvanize against the tangible treat. How do you measure something like that beforehand? It remains the case that the balance of power is very hard to measure.

Note also that, if, like Mearsheimer, we think of power as the assets and resources of a state, it is a short step to thinking about that state as the sum of its assets and resources. Here we have the reason why it lies so close to hand to think of the balance of power as a balance between (great) powers. Here we also have one reason why some of us are unhappy about realism's understanding of power, for, to social theorists, power is a relation between agents, as distinct from the capabilities a particular agent can muster.

The second basic problem with measuring power is that power does not actually reside in the assets and resources themselves. Assets and resources are simply tools for making some other agent do what that agent would not otherwise have done (or, inversely, to abstain from something that agent would otherwise have done). This, you will recall from the previous chapter, is why Clausewitz saw the essence of war as being about breaking the other party's will. *Power is relational*, and a relation has to be instantiated or performed. You may guess at how well or badly an armed force may perform by looking at its former engagements, at its training patterns, and so on, but, in principle, you may know all there is to know about assets and resources at some party's disposal, and also about that party's intentions, and still not be able to guess how the deployment of those assets and resources against you or somebody else will play out and affect their fighting spirit. Anyone who has ever followed a sports team knows that. This is why Geoffrey Blainey argued some years back that since the calculation of power is very hard, the balance of power is not quite known before wars: it is only after wars that the pecking order, the "orderly ladder of power between victors and losers" (Blainey 1973, 19), is known, and the balance agreed upon—for a while.

Blainey captures a key aspect of the balance of power—it is about hierarchy. It is great powers that do the balancing. An interesting question, then, is how much of a states system is included in balancing acts at any one time. One could argue that imperialism was not only a hunt for new resources and more glory, but that it was also a process by which European powers tried to balance one another by taking over new tracts of land. Recall from chapter 4 how, in his 1915 work *Imperialism: The Highest Stage of Capitalism*, Lenin argued that capitalist states could cooperate if they were roughly balanced in strength—that is, if the balance of power was perceived to be fairly stable—but that once that balance was upset, war would break out. Capitalist competition drove them to expand, until their competition enveloped the globe. Then, when war broke out, it would be global (Lenin wrote this as an explanation of the First World War). Imperialism was, therefore, not only a stage of capitalism, but its highest, in the sense of last, stage.

Lenin turned out to be wrong about capitalism, but his perspective on imperialism as driven among other things by a European great power impulse to balance one another not only inside Europe, but globally, has proved analytically fruitful, and his basic idea that a change in equilibrium would bring the danger of war is by now a stock-in-trade of all variants of realism. Defensive realists like Kenneth Waltz think that the system will produce standoffs between great powers—they will act defensively—whereas offensive realists like Mearsheimer (2014) think that the default option of great powers is to increase their power.[1] Today, realists are at one, however, in seeing balancing as the central mechanism of great power politics. Great powers do not appease, that is, give away something in order to keep the rest, and they do not bandwagon, that is, support or even gang up with another great power. They balance, which means that they try to stem the accumulation of power of other states. As noted above, balance of power started as a liberal concept. However, for the last century or so, it has been a realist concept.

A Sigh

The history of ideas about the balance of power is confusing. Three points stand out. First, the balance of power started life in a setting of an emergent European states system. It was then a concept that celebrated the public interest, against any attempt by one power to establish universal hegemony. As an aristocratic politics of passion increasingly gave way to a bourgeois politics of interests, the balance of power shifted referent—that is, it shifted what kind of agents it was attached to. Instead of being about the public interest—the abstract public or common interest of all political entities—it became a term for *raison d'état*, that is, the interests of specific states, which were held to coincide. All states could agree that they liked the balance of power when it was understood as a concept that guaranteed the importance of state interests for politics.

Here is where it gets tricky, though, for in the mid-19th century, an intraliberal and intrabourgeois debate erupted as Manchester liberals like Richard Cobden *attacked* the balance of power. Why would they do such a thing? Because they were looking for a new public interest, and the balance of power certainly was not that any more. Cobden's ideal was that states should have as little contact as possible, and that the peoples of the world should have as much contact as possible. Balance of power was a state thing, and so bad. Free trade, however, Cobden saw as a people-to-people thing, and so good. Hence the attack on the balance of power. The attack had some success, notably that Cobden's view of it as a chimera won the day in legal discourse. At the end of the 19th century, it came to be held as too much of a political concept to serve as a basis for legal thinking, and so it no longer remained a legal term. That did not stop it from remaining a key political concept, however. It remains a problem for all concerned about how to measure it, but to interest-based, state-focused thinking, the concept of the balance of power remains absolutely central to this day.

Key Questions

When we talk about the balance of power, what power is to be balanced?

Is the balance of power naturally occurring?

Note

1. Note that "defensive" and "offensive" realism are terms that Mearsheimer, the self-proclaimed offensive realist, employs to differentiate himself from Waltz, the alleged defensive realist.

Bibliography

Andersen, Morten. 2016. "The Balance of Power." PhD thesis, London School of Economics.

Blainey, Geoffrey. 1973. *The Causes of War*. New York: Free Press.

Boucoyannis, Deborah. 2007. "The International Wanderings of a Liberal Idea, or Why Liberals Can Learn to Stop Worrying and Love the Balance of Power." *Perspectives on Politics* 5 (4): 703–27.

Burke, Edmund. [1790] 1982. *Reflections on the Revolution in France*. Harmondsworth: Penguin.

Hirschman, Albert O. 1997. *The Passions and Interests: Political Arguments for Capitalism before Its Triumph*. Princeton: Princeton University Press.

Khaldoun, Ibn. [1377] 2015. *The Muqaddimah: An Introduction to History*. Princeton: Princeton University Press.

Lenin, Vladimir I. [1915] 2010. *Imperialism: The Highest Stage of Capitalism*. Harmondsworth: Penguin.

Mearsheimer, John. 2014. *The Tragedy of Great Power Politics*. 2nd ed. New York: Norton.

Porter, Theodore M. 1996. *Trust in Numbers: The Pursuit of Objectivity in Science and Public Life*. Princeton: Princeton University Press.

16 ✦ International Law and Human Rights

Conceptual emphasis on international law	Period
ius gentium	Roman and Christian
Natural law	16th century to high modernity
Positive law	high modernity
Human rights	20th century

From a sociological perspective, law is a way of stylizing social conflict so that it becomes easier to deal with. The Romans even made the existence of law definitional for society. They held that where there is society, there is law (Lat. *ubi societas, ibi ius*), and a number of theorists have made this their starting point for thinking about society. That is not, I think, warranted, for it means equating law with written law, and that is probably a mistake—preliterate societies also have institutionalized rules whose breaches are sanctioned by preordained means. For example, in the Eurasian steppe, a man who did not share his food with other members of his group could be put to death by anyone who felt like doing so, and that would, in principle, be the end of the story. But let's start with the Romans, who talked about there being a *ius gentium*, a law of the peoples, with *gentium* being genitive plural of Lat. *gens*, ethnos or people. In the Middle Ages, this was further elaborated as natural law. International law was thus understood as customary law, that is, law that has appeared in the form of usage, stylized practices if you will, but also, and increasingly, as religiously sanctioned. The key thing for our purposes is that, just as there existed in Western Europe a pope who lent institutional religious unity to Western Christendom, so there existed a body of law that supposedly regulated social behavior within Western Christendom.

Development of International Law

With the emergence of states in the 16th and 17th centuries, this collective body of law gave way to ever more refined national bodies of law. *Ius gentium* was under attack as a common framework. At the same time, the discovery of the "New World" posed a new challenge to lawyers: What was the legal status of the inhabitants of the New World and which, if any, laws pertained to them? While all lawyers worried about the impact on *ius gentium* of the emergence of new and specific bodies of state law, it was Spanish lawyers, and particularly Francisco de Vitoria and Francisco Suárez of the so-called Salamanca school, who first and foremost grappled with the situation in the "new world."

What emerged as the replacement of *ius gentium* was *ius inter gentes*, law between peoples. *Ius gentium* did not make a clear distinction between whether things happened on the inside or the outside of the state, but treated law as anchored in nature (natural law) and as it emerged and was accepted (customary law), regardless of subject matter, as one. Boundaries between polities were not a focus. In the 17th and 18th centuries, full-time and secular lawyers emerged, and they were able to establish the exorbitant privilege of having their writings taken as the very base of the emergent international law. To this day, international lawyers are in this interesting position that their scholarship often becomes the basis for subsequent practice. Here we have a particularly clear example of how power and knowledge are intertwined: knowledge production becomes the basis for passing legal judgment, and legal judgments make people do what they otherwise would not have done, which is the basic definition of power. The three names to remember are Hugo Grotius (Dutch, 1583–1645), Samuel Pufendorff (German, 1632–94) and Emer de Vattel (Swiss, 1714–67), who all wrote on a whole range of matters pertaining to relations between states, such as war, trade, and so on.

As noted in chapter 8 above, conceptual historian Reinhart Koselleck stresses how the period 1750–1850 is the period when our modern concepts emerge. This seems to hold where law is concerned. From around 1750, we see a growing chasm between two kinds of knowledge production in general. On the one hand, there was the old-style pontificating on life, the universe, and everything, for which God was the measure of all things. On the other, there was a new, well, newer, style of writing on specifics, which uses *man as the measure of all things* (to quote an old Sophist aphorism that came back in vogue with the Renaissance). "Man" as seen by this new thinking was not Renaissance Man, however, but a calculating individual that looks increasingly like Liberal Man. What we see here is nothing less than the firming up of modern science. In the area of law, we see a movement away from natural law toward positive law, that is, human-made law. The idea that humans make law was of course not new. The newness of what happened from the middle of the 18th century onward resided in the idea that there were no moorings between law made by humans and God. Science does not require a god to work. The Enlightenment evolved a European public law, which was explicitly positivist, that is, it is human-made and does not claim to be morally universal, only part of a specific legal system. It is, I think, no coincidence that the University of Göttingen was particularly important here, for that university was a Saxon university, and so under British sway.[1] The British were, and I would say remain, particularly commonsensical and down to earth in their thinking, be that legal or otherwise. It was indeed a Brit, Jeremy Bentham, who was not only in the forefront when what we now call legal positivism emerged, but who also delivered the perhaps most stinging dictum against natural law ever, when he famously referred to it as "nonsense upon stilts." So, the first thing to note is that international law goes from being basically natural to becoming basically positive. This sparked a philosophical crisis for international law that is still around, for with the foundations that were nature and religion gone, what should be the new foundation? Should it be simply to comfort humans with the thought that at least there was such a thing as law? Or should it perhaps be to point the way toward a bright new future? International law ended up between apology and utopia, to use a book title by Finnish legal scholar Martti Koskenniemi (1989).

In another book called *The Gentle Civilizer of Nations*, Koskenniemi (2001) traces how, from the 1870s onward, international law entered a seemingly progressive phase. A new generation of lawyers basically buried European public law, and put in its stead a legal activism, that is, they wanted to show states the way toward a more well-ordered world, rather than to codify already existing state practice. Here we have a general legal dilemma. Sociologically, the point of law is to introduce a language and an institution that may not only maintain social order but may also reconcile seemingly irreconcilable structural conflicts by attacking single and individualized events. Put more starkly, law tries to bury social conflict in abstruse language and procedures. So, for international law, an evergreen will be: Shall we just put on a Band-Aid, or shall we attempt a cure by not only picking up the pieces after fighting states, but rather prescribe some prophylactic medication? The new lawyers of the late 19th century definitely went for the latter. Not even the Great War really deterred them—the activism continued. And to top it all, while European lawyers were busy thinking about the European states system, they did not really spend all that much energy thinking about the phenomenon of colonialism.

Spread

As Europe became more entangled with the rest of the world, there was a bifurcation in thinking about international law. Legal thinking concentrated explicitly on Europe; it becomes European—as distinct from international—law.

In the 19th century, this division between Europe on the one hand and the rest of the world on the other was further institutionalized through the so-called standard of civilization. We have already met this doctrine, which held that only large-scale polities based on the rule of law were full subjects under international law (see chapter 3). Large-scale polities without the rule of law were considered not civilized, but barbarian, and small-scale polities without the rule of law were considered savage. Places that had no large-scale political organization were held to be *terra nullius*, ownerless land, which is to say that they were up for grabs. Not surprisingly, lawyers from the world's largest empire ever, Britons like James Lorimer and John Westlake, most eagerly codified this legitimation of colonization. As Gerry Simpson (2004) has demonstrated, great powers have proved quite adept at arrogating to themselves more rights than have other states.

Westlake also played an important part in the professionalization of international law as an academic pursuit. In *The Gentle Civilizer of Nations*, which has the telling subtitle *The Rise and Fall of International Law, 1870–1960*, Koskenniemi details how a group of liberals from all over Western Europe set up a new shop, the Institut de Droit International (Institute of International Law). It started out in Ghent, but has since moved around with whoever was elected its secretary general. This institute became the center for a movement to civilize or tame international relations. As seen from outside of Europe in particular, that is, from the point of view of those who suddenly found themselves described as barbarians and savages, the results were mostly unfortunate. Lawyers codified a "standard of civilization," and the attempt to outlaw war that we discussed in chapter 14 must be understood as part and parcel of a wider liberal project of progress. Koskenniemi ends his book in 1960, for by then decolonization was largely over (with major exceptions, the most important being perhaps the Portuguese and Soviet Empires) and the tenor of general political debate had turned away from its focus on progress and toward power.

Human Rights

Besides the demise of the standard of civilization, the key development in international law over the last hundred years is arguably the emergence of human rights. The consolidation of international humanitarian law must be understood as yet another wave of legal activism by mostly Western lawyers. That is, of course, simply an empirical observation; it does not in and of itself tell us anything about the desirability of the phenomenon.

To say that a right is a human right is to say that it pertains to somebody simply by dint of biology—it comes with being a member of the species. Note that universality is of the essence here—it does not matter what kind of human or what you have done (such as water boarding someone for fun, mowing down 69 people including 33 children attending a political summer camp, or burning a fellow human being alive in a cage, to take some recent and well-publicized examples), you are still a human and so your human rights cannot be forfeited. As Lynn Hunt (2007, 20) puts it:

> Human rights are natural, in the sense of simply coming with being human; they are equal, in that they pertain to everybody in the same way and the same degree; and they are universal, in that everybody has them, regardless of biological or social attributes or of what one may have perpetrated.

There is a sense in which the universality of religious-based natural law is perpetuated by substituting biology for religion here. Note also that, if a right is a human right, it trumps what states can do. To take but one contentious issue, if bare life is a human right (a European view), then the death penalty, which is practiced in many places on the globe, is in breach of human rights. Human rights is a hefty challenge not only to international law as it stood before international human rights law started to grow, but to the logic of the entire international society, for it brings back the basic thought in *ius gentium*, that law applies regardless of boundaries, that humans are humans regardless of citizenship, biological niceties, or where on the planet they happen to be. This is a return of universalism to international law, and so a challenge to *ius inter gentes*.

IR study of human rights is dominated by "thin" constructivists. As noted in chapter 9, constructivists stress how society emerges out of human actions, and thin constructivists think in terms of norms. A norm is a standard that lays down what is appropriate behavior for an actor with a certain identity in a certain situation. Thin constructivists think of norms in terms of "life cycles," which is to say that norms are introduced, then they spread (or, to use the rather histrionic wording of thin constructivists, "cascade"), and then they are internalized by agents. This internalization—the making of norms into something unthinking, something one just does, that is, doxa—is the result of socialization, the practice of having thrust upon one and taking up social norms and making them one's own. The process passes through two tipping points or thresholds. First, at some point, the norm in question spreads so widely that it can begin to be internalized. Second, at some later point, so many people internalize the norm that it becomes a standard part of the repertoire for what to do in a certain social circle or indeed an entire society. Note that this way of thinking about norms presupposes a specific theory of action. Individuals do not act in order to maximize resources, that is, they do not follow a "logic of consequence," but they act by doing the done, expected, and right thing, which is to say that they follow a "logic of appropriateness" (March and Olsen 1989). It is this view of human action as socially determined, that is, determined by specific norms, that is the hallmark of the thin constructivist (by contrast, a "thick" constructivist does not talk about norms, but about power).

There is an obvious logic to why thin constructivists concentrate on human rights, for human rights may be understood as a bundle of norms— the norm upholds the right. Take the right to life, which is basic. It is upheld by the norm that life shall not be taken. It is fairly easy to trace the life cycle of this norm, from its introduction, specifically in religious thinking of many strands, via its global spread (note the huge number of setbacks) to its internalization. Note that internalization (in individuals) often goes hand in hand with institutionalization (in society) of the norm, in the form of making norms into law. In the case of human rights law, it has only blossomed in the post–Cold War period. The UN established a

High Commissioner for Human Rights in 1993. There was the establishment of the International Criminal Court, which began its work in 2002. The point here is not that there were no precedents—humanitarian law has been around for well over a century, and in the aftermath of the Second World War, groups of lawyers at Harvard, Paris, and London were instrumental in developing it—but we would do well to pause and ask ourselves why it took an entire reconfiguration of the international states system for international human rights to emerge (Hoffmann 2010). The importance of this change in the power configuration inside which human rights were institutionalized forces a question: Are thin constructivists right in focusing on the individual level and foregrounding the role of norms for social change, or should we rather follow thick constructivists and focus on the social level and power relations? You will see by the way I set up this question that my answer would be that power should be foregrounded. That does not mean that a focus on norms is unwarranted. Any social order is dependent on people upholding it, and internalization of norms is certainly a way for this to happen. The question is rather about the way internalization and institutionalization take place—does this happen as a result of argument and conviction only, or is power afoot? Were there not structures in place, put there by states themselves, *before* legal scholars and activists came onstream? Aren't activists simply not only tolerated but also actively used by states?

Consider once again a particularly well-received book on norms, Margaret Keck and Kathryn Sikkink's *Activists beyond Borders*, on so-called transnational activists. A key factor for Keck and Sikkink (1998, 13) is what they call the boomerang model, where local activists who have no recourse to their own government work with activists across their borders, and then these activists target that government indirectly, through international NGOs, INGOs, and other states. Keck and Sikkink (1998, 16–25) identify four particularly effective (and modular) strategies or policies that transnational organization networks have used to bring about change. The first is about politicizing previously unproblematized social practices so that they become problems to be discussed rather than stuff taken for granted. This is agenda-setting. The second strategy is about symbols—it turns on finding some kind of hook, some way of speaking about the issue that activists want to make into a problem, that speaks to as broad a global public as possible. As an example, they offer violence against women, which activist groups first framed as a question of human rights. That certainly spoke to a global audience. Once the issue was placed firmly on the agenda and had become part of legal discourse, however, some activists started to ask themselves if a change of frame from legal discourse to health discourse would not bring even more enhanced impetus to the question of violence against women. I note this example because it brings out that activists do not necessarily rest on their laurels once Keck and Sikkink's modular cycle is finished—they may go on for yet another round in a new policy area.

If politicization and framing are important strategies, so are the third and the fourth strategies noted by Keck and Sikkink, namely what they call leverage—that is, linking the issue to other issues (development aid being a typical example), or shaming the culprit state in various arenas and outlets. Finally, there is accountability, which is about getting governments to commit to a certain principle by signing treaties, changing laws, launching information campaigns, and so on. Once a government is committed, strategies like shaming become even more potent, for the charge against a given government is no longer limited to pointing out that they should adopt a certain policy, but changes to being the much more troubling, because immanent, charge that governments should stick to what they themselves have announced as being their very own policies.

Two kinds of issues seem to lend themselves particularly well to transnational campaigning. It is no coincidence that the first one falls squarely in the human rights category, while the other one concerns jurisprudence, and, more specifically, the principle of equality before the law.

Bodily harms that are readily traced directly to a specific group of perpetrators lend themselves particularly well to transnational campaigns, as do issues involving legal equality of opportunity. Why equality of opportunity should have transcultural resonance is not completely clear. However, most of the societies where such campaigns are carried out have adopted liberal institutions of democracy and rule of law, yet exclude some significant part of the population from participation in these institutions. This disjuncture between the neutral discourse of equality implicit in liberalism and the unequal access to liberal institutions opens up a space for symbolic political action and the accountability politics of networks. In other words, liberalism carries within it not the seeds of its own destruction, but the seeds of its expansion. Liberalism, with all its historical shortcomings, contains a subversive element that plays into the hands of activists (Keck and Sikkink 1998, 205).

So much for how human rights emerge. Let's move from process to substance: What are human rights? There is, as already noted, the right to bare life, that is, the right to bodily integrity: no murder or cruel and unusual punishment—that is, torture. Following the British historian of ideas Isaiah Berlin (2002, 48), these are often called negative freedoms: "[t]he fundamental sense of freedom is freedom from chains, from imprisonment, from enslavement by others" as he put it; so-called positive freedom took a back seat to this. These positive rights come in three flavors. There are civic rights spearheaded by the Enlightenment—the right to free speech, the freedom of assembly, and so on. Should these be thought of as human rights? And then there are so-called social rights, that is, the right to resources. A "decent life" may be conceived of as including anything from the right to bare life to the right to a life above a certain poverty line to a life on some kind of average global standard. How much of this should be categorized as human rights? During the Cold War, this was a bone of contention between the West and the Soviet Union, with the West championing free speech and the Soviet Union championing social rights. Since the end of the Cold War, activists and international lawyers have put forward a number of other candidates for human rights, so-called third-generation rights (after civic and social). An example of such a candidate would be a (human?) right to a healthy climate.

International lawyers grapple with many of the same problems, as do IR scholars. It would be a mistake for us not to keep an eye on legal discourse, not only for its analytical insights, but perhaps first and foremost because evolving international law seems to be increasingly important in shaping everyday international relations themselves.

Key Questions

Should international law be understood as natural or positive?

Are human rights universal?

Note

1. It was founded in 1737 by Gerlach Adolph von Münchhausen, who was the British king George II's chief minister in Hanover.

Bibliography

Berlin, Isaiah. 2002. *Liberty: Incorporating "Four Essays on Liberty"*. Oxford: Oxford University Press.

Hoffmann, Stefan-Ludwig, ed. 2010. *Human Rights in the Twentieth Century*. Cambridge: Cambridge University Press.

Hunt, Lynn. 2007. *Inventing Human Rights*. New York: Norton.

Keck, Margaret E., and Kathryn Sikkink. 1998. *Activists beyond Borders: Advocacy Networks in International Politics*. Ithaca: Cornell University Press.

Koskenniemi, Martti. 1989. *From Apology to Utopia*. Cambridge: Cambridge University Press.

Koskenniemi, Martti. 2001. *The Gentle Civilizer of Nations: The Rise and Fall of International Law, 1870–1960*. Cambridge: Cambridge University Press.

March, James G., and John P. Olsen. 1989. *Rediscovering Institutions: The Organizational Basis of Politics*. New York: Free Press.

Simpson, Gerry. 2004. *Great Powers and Outlaw States: Unequal Sovereigns in the International Legal Order*. Cambridge: Cambridge University Press.

17 ✦ Power and Sovereignty

Frame of Sovereignty	Period
Mytho-sovereignty	Antique and Christian
Proto-sovereignty	Renaissance
Raison d'ètat sovereignty	Classical Age
Popular sovereignty	Modernity

Since Max Weber, we have thought of power as A's ability to make B do something he would not otherwise have done. In 1974, British sociologist Steven Lukes published a small book called *Power: A Radical View*, where he suggested that there are three dimensions to power. The most obvious, or one-dimensional, analysis concerns what A does to make B do this, that, or the other thing. In chapter 10 on security, the question asked was who secures what against whom, with what, in which way. In terms of power analysis, this is a one-dimensional approach. By way of example of a power grab, in 2015 Russia annexed Crimea, which was a part of Ukraine. The simplest way to analyze this is to say that Russia made Ukraine do what it would not otherwise have done. A number of Russian agents were at work—undercover agents, Crimean criminals, the Russian military, the Russian press—but one way to think of all that is to see these agents simply as derivative of a principal agent, Russia. Russia acted on Ukraine. This would be a one-dimensional analysis of power.

Two Dimensions

If you think other stuff is also relevant, however, you have to push on. A two-dimensional analysis of power focuses not only on the specific sequence of actions, but also on how organizations are mobilized: "All forms of political organisation have a bias in favour of the exploitation of some kinds of conflict and the suppression of others, because organisation is the mobilisation of bias. Some issues are organised into politics while others are organised out" (Schattschneider, quoted in Lukes 1974, 16). For example, in the Crimea takeover, the mobilized personnel came from an organization, the Russian army, whose size and degree of combat-readiness was a power factor in the equation, since it was clearly relevant to why Ukraine did what it would not otherwise have done, namely to pull out of Crimea. The weakness of the Ukrainian army was also a factor. So were the Russian, Ukrainian, and international media, whose reporting on the situation in Ukraine framed the conflict and impinged on the costs and benefits for Ukraine of following different courses of action. We could add a number of other organizations whose existence and practices framed the situation and so were important power nodes for what happened in the Crimea, everything from veterans clubs to the United Nations.

Three Dimensions

The first power dimension concerns actor to actor, and the second power dimension concerns the organizational biases involved in framing the actor-to-actor situation in ways that change either the ease with which A and B may or may not act. Lukes also observes that there are a number of cases where A is able to make B do what he may not otherwise have done on walkover. B does not know what is happening, or does not understand the effects of what is happening before it is too late to avoid doing what he would otherwise not have done. Lukes (1974, 23–24) asks rhetorically:

> Indeed, is it not the supreme exercise of power to get another or others to have the desires you want them to have—that is, to secure their compliance by controlling their thoughts and desires? [. . .] is it not the supreme and most insidious exercise of power to prevent people, to whatever degree, from having grievances by shaping their perceptions, cognitions and preferences in such a way that they accept their role in the existing order of things, either because they can see or imagine no alternative to it, or because they see it as natural and unchangeable, or because they value it as divinely ordained and beneficial?

It is this third dimension that is of particular interest to Lukes the Marxist (you will observe how the Marxian idea of false consciousness is at the heart of it). As for my example, I leave it to you to think through which groups of people who supported the takeover, only to discover that the effect of it was that they had to do things they did not want to do. Note also the role of the Crimean Tatars here. They were the power on the peninsula until 1774, when there was a Russian takeover and an estimated half of the population fled to Turkey. In 1944, Moscow deported the Crimean Tatars to Central Asia. Since the fall of the Soviet Union, they had largely embraced their new Ukrainian citizenships. And yet their voice was suppressed during the takeover. Someone is usually paying the price for social change. The voiceless are generally important groups to look for in power analysis.

Lukes's use of dimensions is elegant. He comes across as three dimensional, whereas many previous scholars are simply one- or two-dimensional. The same kind of rhetorical framing may be turned against Lukes himself, however. One may ask: What about all those situations where it is the general setup of things, that is, structures and not specific individuals (the As), that make us do what we do? What if the very fabric of social life, and not only specific organizations, are set up so that not only B, but also A, do what they otherwise would not have done?

A Fourth Dimension: Governmentality

This is the perspective of French philosopher, historian, and social scientist Michel Foucault. Foucault suggests that the specific way we produce knowledge about the world has effects on how we act and behave. Where there is knowledge, there is power. The slogan "knowledge is power" goes back to early English scientist Francis Bacon (1561–1626), so that in itself is not new. What Bacon had in mind, though, was knowledge as a power resource for A. Foucault, on the other hand, wants to highlight how any social order is suffused with power simply because it is based on certain forms of knowledge production, and not others, and that this is inevitable. Consider Crimea again. As part and parcel of the Russian thrust into Crimea and eastern Ukraine, we saw, and continue to see, knowledge production of a place called "Novorossiya." Russians allegedly constructed this place, and Russians now lay claim to it. Incidentally, it overlaps with Ukrainian areas now claimed by Russians. The production of this kind of knowledge is power, for if we think that historical claims to territory have weight and we acknowledge the historical claim to a "Novorossiya" now being produced, then that changes what may and may not be done in the area. Foucault, however, would be more interested in the preconditions for this. What view of history makes a power grab like the "Novorossiya" narrative possible? This represents a view of history as a weapon, more specifically, as Lenin saw it, a hammer. What kind of power makes it possible that the Russian media reporting on what happens in Crimea and "Novorossiya" is so homogenous? That would be surveillance—state control of Russian media.

To Foucault, power resides in the relation, however asymmetrical, between A and B. It is not something that A "has." Rather, it is intersubjective. Foucault operates with three principal modes of power relations: sovereignty, dominance, and governmentality.

(1) For Foucault, sovereignty is a game between different wills. As a form of power, sovereignty is characterized by the fact that it is not obvious who is going to be master (Foucault contrasts this with domination, where there is no question about this). It is this type of power relations—understood as an ongoing negotiation between subjects regarding who is right and who can dictate the other person's actions, where it is constantly open who is the superior party—that, according to Foucault, is constantly present in relations between human beings.

The strategic action that dominates sovereign power games is central to most analyses of power. Three points should be noted. First, Foucault emphasizes that even though power relations permeate society, society cannot be reduced simply to power relations. He exemplifies this by saying that negotiations about truth with regard to psychiatric medication and mathematics have a value of their own, regardless of the power relations they are incorporated into. Society exists, among other things, by dint of its regimes of truth—if a group of humans do not share a basic understanding of certain basic phenomena, then that group has no coherence, and so cannot be a society. So, regimes of truth are constitutive of societies and polities. This is what French sociologist Émile Durkheim meant when he said that society is despotic (see chapter 2). Foucault would agree.[1] The key point where power is concerned is that knowledge and power are inextricably linked, for knowledge, understood as regimes of truth, constitutes society, and the specific ways of thinking that constitute society make us do stuff we would not otherwise have done.

Second, Foucault mentions explicitly that strategic games could very well be present, for instance, in a study situation. Hence, institutionalization does not necessarily imply that subjects are reduced to docile bodies. This is a central point. Subjects playing sovereignty games are not considered free in the sense that they can think completely outside of, as in independently of, the regimes of truth of their societies. They are only as free as Foucauldian subjects can be, meaning free to act within the regimes of truth that constitute them as subject.

Third, the strategic game between different sovereigns (first the kings themselves, then states understood as collective sovereign subjects) has been the typical form of power in the European states system. The establishment of the states system from the late 15th century and onward is inextricably linked to the increase in relations between sovereigns, built on what has later been called sovereignty. Sovereignty can be understood exactly as a strategic game.

(2) Dominance is a direct type of power relation where there is no question of who the master (Lat. *dominus*) is. In a close reading of Foucault's concept of discipline, Ransom (1997, 57) concludes by defining this as "those micro-mechanisms of power whereby subjects are moulded to serve the needs of power." These practices are specific: a worker by the production line, a soldier in the army, a student in a boarding school. The result of discipline is thus that the individual develops a new ability, making him or her capable of fulfilling a new role or even filling a new subject position. Successful dominance produces what Foucault calls docile bodies.

Dominated subjects may be "free" in a much more limited sense than subjects who are active in sovereign power games. They can, however, offer resistance, for, according to Foucault, there cannot be any power relation without resistance. Where there is only one will that frictionlessly writes its truth onto another, there are no relations, and thus no power. Dominated subjects thus remain free to commit suicide, jump out of the window, murder their masters, and so on. The key point is that regardless of what they do, it will not be sufficient to change who is the master. If we are dealing with a relationship characterized by dominance, the weaker part's actions can never be anything but resistance—resistance toward an order that the subject cannot change by the power of his actions alone.

(3) Governmentality is a type of power relation that comes between dominance and sovereignty, and which is connected to the reflexive—that is, how the self governs itself. Governmentality denotes the conduct of conduct, as Foucault puts it—that is, how things people do are orchestrated by social settings. Both Lukes's second and third dimensions of power

are about this, but Foucault has in mind something more specific, namely how power relations find their way into human bodies that then not only go on to do stuff, but also to think that what they do is *right*. Consider how we raise children. The point is not only that children should do what we say when we tell them, but that they should conduct themselves as we have told them to even when we are not there, and feel good when they do what we have told them to do. Or consider the teacher/student relation: teachers are supposed to try to make students think about stuff not only in the classroom and when they are writing their essays, but all the time—also when they are outside of formal teaching contexts. These are examples of conduct of conduct. They are also examples of trying to get someone to do something they would not otherwise have done, and so these examples denote a mode of power, the mode that Foucault calls governmentality. Governmentality is a mode of power that lies between acting strategically and being dominated, for whenever you attempt to govern yourself, you will seek to draw on a set of technologies that are taken from various fields such as your schooling experience, your experience with having others trying to govern you, from technologies such as exercising, dieting, and praying.

Hence, the reason why Foucault formulates and emphasizes the type of power relation that he calls governmentality is because of its central and understudied role in contemporary postindustrial societies. This is particularly connected with the fact that these human collectives are today characterized by firm institutionalization, where what we call society places itself in between the subjects and the sovereign. The institutionalization of society has a decisive impact on the formation of subjects.

Sovereignty

So, to Foucault, sovereignty is a form of power that works like a game. The Swedish IR scholar Jens Bartelson (1995) starts his analysis of sovereignty in international relations from the Foucauldian view that truth and knowledge are all produced discursively, which is to say, in a social field where power is ever-present because it comes from everywhere. It follows that social phenomena like sovereignty are emergent, which means that they have no essence, but take their meaning from the ongoing contestation of how to fix their meaning. That the process is ongoing does not mean that it is continuous; new positions are built up over time, and tend to assert their dominance swiftly, thus causing breaks in the meaning of concepts. In his book *A Genealogy of Sovereignty* (1995), however, Bartelson sees sovereignty as what frames politics, that is, something that sets politics off from other nonpolitical stuff and so delineates politics, but which is not itself either political or nonpolitical. Sovereignty frames politics, just like a frame (Greek *parergon*) frames a picture. The modern way to do this was to invest sovereignty in the people of a state: the frame of politics equals the boundary of the nation-state, and sovereignty is the state of having no one from outside dictate what happens inside of that boundary.

In order to bring out what the ontological status of a phenomenon thus understood is, Bartelson leans on a comparison of fire and sovereignty. Fire used to be treated, with air, water, and soil, as one of the four basic elements. However, when physics turned to understanding the world in terms of molecules and thermodynamic laws, fire went up in smoke within scientific discourse. There was a break. In many other discourses, however, fire stayed on. The methodological lesson seems clear. Since phenomena have no essence, our job as analysts is to demonstrate how they are produced socially. Sovereignty, or fire, or any concepts for that matter, cannot be fanned down to an "essence," legal or otherwise, for it only exists in its various incarnations in discourse. It follows that there is nothing to look for outside discourse.

But isn't fire an apolitical term, and sovereignty a political one? In certain discourses, yes, but ask Buddhists in Tibet, among whom self-immolation is a key form of protest against Chinese imperialism, or fundamentalist Christian theologians, who dwell on the nature of hell. To them, fire is deeply political. The methodological point here is simple: anything may become a political term, for drawing the distinction between what is political and what is not political is itself a political act (a good example here is 1970s Western feminist discussions, where enormous amounts of energy were spent on arguing that the private is political). Bartelson (1995, 6) gives us a productive methodological chestnut when he suggests that the process just discussed may be understood in terms of asking three questions:

If knowledge is understood as a system for the formation of valid statements, all knowledge is knowledge about differentiation, and this differentiation is a political activity. First, in order to constitute itself as such, some given knowledge must demarcate itself from what [. . .] is not knowledge, be it opinion, ideology or superstition. Second [. . .] knowledge implies a set of ontological decisions: what does exist, and what does not exist [. . .] From these decisions, two other decisions follow. One is ethical, and tells us who we are, who is a friend, who is an enemy and who is a stranger. In short, the ethical decision is one of deciding who is Same and who is Other. The other decision is meta-historical, and tells us where we came from, how we became friends, how we got here, where we are, and where we are heading. In short, knowledge, being political to the extent that it differentiates, is indissolubly intertwined with identity and history.

It follows that the questions to ask in order to understand a phenomenon like sovereignty include how an epoch defines knowledge vs. nonknowledge (e.g., a god guarantees sovereignty); what exists (e.g., a people that may then be conceptualized as the keeper of sovereignty); who we are (e.g., slaves, subjects, citizens); and where we are in history (e.g., on our way to subjugate more territory under our sovereign rule). Cambridge historian Harry Hinsley's (1966, 1) conceptualization of sovereignty as "the idea that there is a final and absolute political authority in the political community and [. . .] no final and absolute authority exists elsewhere" captures the centrality of how a strengthened distinction between the inside and outside of states was key to the shift. By the same token, Bartelson (1995, 4) highlights how sovereignty "forms the crucial link between [international] anarchy and [domestic] hierarchy." We may ask exactly when this shift took place. The answer given is often the Peace of Westphalia (1648), for it is often alleged that it was here the principle was enshrined in a treaty. It is, however, always risky to peg a long drawn-out process that enshrines a principle on one specific event. We are on safer ground if we think of sovereignty as an emergent concept that frames relations between states in different ways in different periods. It is arguable that sovereignty only became a full-fledged framing principle of state relations after the Napoleonic Wars. It is also arguable that the period leading up to the Peace of Westphalia and the discussion of whether the principle of *cuius regio eius religio*—subjects should have the same religion as their king—is key.

One may also, however, find a prehistory of the principle, where the stress is less on the differentiation of the inside from the outside, and more on the status of the sovereign leader as someone who can do what he wants. By these lights, in the Eurasian steppe, and also in sedentary territories adjacent to it, sovereignty was a question of having God on your side. If you won battles, it meant that God was smiling at you. In the European Middle Ages, this changed. Sovereignty became a question of how the institution of kingship as such, as distinct from who was actually filling that institution at any one time, was of God. With the French Revolution, the consecrating agent of sovereignty shifted from God to the people—so-called popular (from Lat. *populus*, people) sovereignty. Rule in the name of God became less important as a legitimating strategy, whereas rule in the name of the people became more important. A key drama of the 19th century was how two great powers—France and Great Britain—operated mainly on the basis of popular sovereignty, whereas the crowned heads of the three other great powers—Russia, Austria-Hungary, and Prussia—stuck to the old thinking and continued to look to God for legitimation of their sovereign status.

In a follow-up book to *A Genealogy of Sovereignty*, Bartelson (2014) argues that we are approaching a new break, with sovereignty no longer being invested in the nation-state. The frame is moving to enframe specific ways of doing politics that qualify those who pursue such politics as being sovereign, and disqualify those who fall outside of that new frame. Sovereignty becomes something endowed by the collective of states, rather than being something that resides in the people of a specific polity. This would be a new usage, and it would have very important consequences, for it would lay down that sovereignty is something that is actually granted on a continual basis by the international society of states. That is a rather different way of understanding sovereignty from the modern way, which was that there were no one above the sovereign, for it would mean that the society of states is indeed above the sovereign. The effects of such a change in meaning are enormous, not least in terms of intervention, which is the topic of the following chapter. One particularly conducive IR debate to consult in this regard is the one on failed states. If "failed" means nonsovereign, and if the place where "failure" is decided is among the society of states, then the shift is here. States, beware: failure is in the eye of the beholder. If international society should come to decide which polities are worthy of being sovereign, it would lead to a highly significant change in international relations at large.

Key Questions

How many dimensions of power do we really need to understand international relations?

Was sovereignty born in Augsburg in 1555, in Westphalia in 1648, in Vienna in 1815, or none of the above?

Note

1. However, where Durkheim would stress the necessity of this despotism, Foucault would see it as the job of the intellectual to demonstrate exactly how society is despotic, and what effects that has, not least regarding which groups will pay the price for what specific form of despotism. As an example of such effects, consider how debates about subalterns tend to cluster around race in the United States, class in Britain, and sexual minorities in Russia. All three *problematiques* exist in all three states, but they are weighted differently, and, as a result, different groups will be advantaged and disadvantaged in different ways.

Bibliography

Bartelson, Jens. 1995. *A Genealogy of Sovereignty*. Cambridge: Cambridge University Press.

Bartelson, Jens. 2014. *Sovereignty as Symbolic Form*. London: Routledge.

Hinsley, F. H. 1966. *Sovereignty*. New York: Basic.

Lukes, Steven. 1974. *Power: A Radical View*. London: Palgrave.

Ransom, John S. 1997. *Foucault's Discipline: The Politics of Subjectivity*. Durham, NC: Duke University Press.

18 ✦ Intervention: Military, Economic, Humanitarian

Kind of Intervention (modular)	Period
Land grabs	Comes with large-scale polities–
Popular intervention	1790s–
Responsibility to Protect	1990s–

Inter means "between" and *venere* means "to come." To intervene, then, is to come between, to interpose oneself. In order to separate intervention off from other concepts such as occupation and war, it is helpful to consider temporality. One cannot interpose oneself forever. An intervention must be of limited duration. A land grab by one polity against another is an intervention, and it ends either with retreat or with occupation (and then perhaps incorporation) of the land grabbed. The point in time when the intervention is over and the occupation begins is either when the status quo ante (the situation as it was before the intervention) is reestablished, or when the kerfuffle dies down. Interventions are also limited in terms of use of force. If a polity throws everything it has on something, or if the entire future of a polity is on the line, it is war, not intervention. Therefore, Iraq's attempted land grab of Kuwait in 1990 was a question of the incorporation of Kuwait into Iraq. The action was more than an intervention, and was treated accordingly by third parties. We talk about it as the Gulf War because Kuwait's future as a sovereign entity was at stake, but we talk about the US intervention in the war (or, more colloquially, about the invasion of Kuwait) because the US military operation was of limited duration and did not concern the very future of the United States in any ontically meaningful way.

Polities meddle in one another's business all the time, in the form of travel, trade, and a host of other social interactions (Finnemore 2003). This chapter will focus on military intervention, that is, intervention by directly coercive means by regular soldiers or their functional equivalent (function here means task, so functional equivalent simply means similar ways of getting the task done, such as using personnel that is not regular or trained local personnel). I should like to note, however, that there are also such things as political intervention and economic intervention. Direct economic interventions are of two kinds: sanctions and embargoes. Economic sanctions try to deny a polity the possibility of exporting goods and capital (and, theoretically, labor), whereas embargoes try to deny a polity the possibility of importing goods and capital (and, theoretically, labor). Economic sanctions are flimsy things. As Katherine Barbieri and Jack Levy (1999) have demonstrated, states tend to maintain trading relations even when they are at war. They sometimes do have effect, however, not least symbolically. A key case in the literature is economic sanctions by the West against the Apartheid regime of South Africa in the 1980s and early 1990s, which, arguably, contributed to its fall.

It is a transhistorical phenomenon that people meddle in other people's business, so in order for the concept of military intervention to be useful for IR, we first have to ask exactly what an external polity comes between when it intervenes. In chapter 2 above, the point was made that a state has three key elements—a territory, subjects, and an administration. To intervene means to come between some of these elements. Exactly which elements is a question of historical variation.

In order to demonstrate how this works, let me give you an example from Afghanistan, or more precisely, the city of Balkh, which in 1006 put up stiff resistance to a Qarakhanid invasion, which we might now categorize as an intervention. In the end the city fell. It was pillaged and the sultan-owned bazaar was burned to the ground. The displaced sultan, Mahmut of Ghazni, soon drove the invaders out, and berated the people of Balkh for defending their city:

> What do subjects have to do with war? It is natural that your town was destroyed and that they burnt property belonging to me, which had brought in such revenues. You should be required to pay an indemnity for the losses, but we pardoned you; only see to it that it does not happen again: if any king (at a given moment) proves himself stronger, and requires taxes and protects you, you must pay taxes and thereby save yourselves. (quoted in Bartold 1968)

Why does this sound so quaint, perhaps even shocking, today? Because we expect the intervention of a would-be conqueror to take place between a ruler and his administrative apparatus, on the one hand, and a people, on the other. Here, however, we have an example of a ruler who objects not to the attempt at usurping his subjects, but his territory and its infrastructure. "The people" does not enter into it (except as purveyors of goods and services, but purveyors who are thought of as easily dispensable).

We should not be shocked, for this was the order of the day everywhere, until things began to change at the extreme Western end of the Eurasian continent. Subjects became people and people became population. The idea that groups of subjects had political rights is an old one. The idea that all subjects as a whole have rights, however, began to form slowly, hovered somewhere in the wings of England's so-called Glorious Revolution in 1688, and came into its own with full force only with the French and American Revolutions.

Intervention and "The People"

Note, however, that there is something fishy about the concept of "the people" in both these revolutionary cases. In France, the revolution turns on the concept of the "third estate." Estates were ranks of the population, a mix of professions and classes if you like, with the first estate being the clergy, the second the aristocracy, and the third the rest: peasants, burghers (the bourgeoisie), and, well, the badly dressed really, the sansculottes.[1] Women were basically sorted by their fathers and husbands (with a main problem being what happened when the two differed in status). "The people" of the French Revolution were not just everybody. Before the coming of modernity in the mid-1700s, the people were the aristocracy. "The people," then, became a concept that was used to denote a certain group that wanted more rights. In the 18th century, including what happened in Revolutionary France, despite the strivings of the sansculottes, it was the bourgeoisie that was able to mobilize the concept of "the people" as a fighting concept. It was the same with the American Revolution. Some of the very same individuals who pontificated about "We, the people" doing this, that, or the other thing were slave owners. As in France, women were not even in the running for being part of "the people." "The people" is one of these concepts that we should be extremely wary of, for historically that moniker is always a shibboleth for a specific group. In today's political landscape, it tends to be used about a badly defined majority, and is arguably always excluding of certain groups. Contemporary American examples of such groups would be illegal immigrants and the four million people who are under constant surveillance (with half of that being the country's prison population).

The key interest of the concept of the people to the concept of intervention has to do not with the noun people, but with one of the adjectives that is derived from that noun, namely popular. As discussed in the previous chapter, the emergence of ever more representation in Britain and in postrevolutionary France ushered in the idea that sovereignty is vested in the people, and not in the king. This makes for a change in the concept of the state, for if a state is a constellation consisting of territory, subjects, and administration, then any change in how one thinks about the relationship between and the relative importance of these three entities will change the meaning of the concept of the state. The crucial thing in terms of intervention is that the foreign party that intervenes now comes between the rulers (king, president, state administration) and the people, and that this is considered wrong by those who think that popular sovereignty should be the order of the day. Here we have the reason that the old Afghan example comes across as shocking: it reads out the people, whereas many now think that the people should be the backbone of the state.

One of the things that the Congress of Europe that was formed after the Napoleonic Wars dealt with was putting down rebellions by means of military intervention. These rebellions tended to be staged by the bourgeoisie of some city in the name of popular sovereignty. For example, when the Concert met in Verona in 1822, one of the items on the agenda was what was happening in Spain. In 1820, a city rebellion had spread, with the result that Spain now had a liberal regime. The Congress decided that France, the only great power to border on Spain and at this point a country that had had enough of revolution for a while, was free to intervene to support Spanish royalists and put an end to the liberal regime. The intervention was successful, and the three-year-long liberal reign (Sp. Trienio Liberal) came to an end.[2]

I hope you have smelled a rat here. On the one hand, there is supposed to be a principle of popular sovereignty, and, on the other, there is an intervention against a popular uprising by France that takes place on behalf of the crowned head of Spain, and with the blessing of the crowned heads of the great powers. You smelled correctly. The legitimacy principle of popular sovereignty was weak everywhere except in Britain. Actually, Britain's objection to intervention against popular uprisings in the name of royal legitimacy was the key factor in bringing an end to the formal meetings of the Concert of Europe. In 1848, when revolutions broke out all over Europe, it was left to specific great powers to intervene, as did Russia in Hungary in 1849. During the 19th century, intervention was a term used in relation to regime types: Should there be interventions against or on behalf of liberal regimes? If you have a vague feeling that there is something familiar about this *problematique*, I'd say you are right again. The clearest 19th century argument against intervention, John Stuart Mill's essay from 1859 (1973), *A Few Words on Non-Intervention*, puts the argument that democracy cannot be imposed by intervention from without, but has to come from within.[3]

The later 19th- and early 20th-century Russian revolutionaries were obsessed with the French Revolution. They thought history moved on rails, and saw their own revolution as a replay of the French Revolution. To some degree, they themselves saw to it that it was. For example, the concept of the people was used in the same way. Again, "the people" (Rus. *narod*) as used by the Russian revolutionaries was not a universal term. Aristocrats, merchants, even prosperous peasants (*kulaks*) were not part of it. "The people" consisted of minor peasants, workers, and sailors and soldiers with the right class-consciousness. "The People's" will was by definition the same as the will of the Communist Party. In this situation, liberal states, what the Russian revolutionaries always referred to as capitalist states, intervened on the side of the counterrevolutionaries (*Whites*). Once again, we see that changes in the concept of the people spawned a new understanding of the state, and that a new understanding of the state spawns intervention. The same cadences surrounded the Chinese Revolution of the 1940s.

During the Cold War, intervention remained a term tied to regimes, as the two superpowers, the United States and the Soviet Union, intervened throughout the globe, and particularly in their own mutually acknowledged "spheres of interest," in order to see to it that other states remained in their camps. US military interventions included Cuba (the abortive Bay of Pigs intervention in 1961), the Dominican Republic (1965), Grenada (1983), and, arguably and more indirectly, Nicaragua (the early 1980s). Soviet military interventions included Hungary (1956), Czechoslovakia (1968), Afghanistan (1979, turned into a war), and, arguably and more indirectly, Poland (1956 and 1981).

Humanitarian Intervention

There were examples of military interventions of another kind during the Cold War, so-called humanitarian interventions, where the alleged goal of the intervention was not to change the regime type of the polity intervened against, but to put an end to atrocities. Two key examples are Vietnam's intervention in Pol Pot's Cambodia in 1978 and Tanzania's intervention in Idi Amin's Uganda in 1979. With hindsight, it lies close to hand to see these as valiant undertakings, but, at the time, they were highly controversial. There is a good reason for this, which is that there is no such thing as a purely altruistic intervention. The intervening polity always has other fish to fry in addition to putting an end to atrocities.

This *problematique* has been at the forefront of international relations in the quarter century after the end of the Cold War, and even became a question of law from 2005 on, when the United Nation passed a resolution on states' "Responsibility to Protect" the human rights of their citizens and the international community's responsibility to prevent major human rights violations. How should we refer to the US-led operations in Serbia, Afghanistan, Iraq, and Libya? Here we have a good example of how the use of concepts is deeply political. The 1999 bombing of Serbia was definitely an intervention and not a war, for it was of limited duration and limited force was used. Was it a humanitarian intervention, though, as the United States maintained, or was it an intervention to get rid of a particular regime, which would, as we have seen, make it akin to inventions as they have evolved over the last two centuries? The same kinds of controversies surround the US-led Libya campaign in 2011.

US operations in Afghanistan and Iraq also began as interventions, directed against regimes. The alleged direct reason for intervening in Iraq in 2003, that a nuclear program was in full flow, turned out to be a canard. President George W. Bush famously had a photo op arranged where he landed a fighter plane on an aircraft carrier with a banner reading "Mission Accomplished"—only for the intervention to turn into a costly war with detrimental consequences that are still in the news. For the record, it should be noted that an almost unanimous corps of US Arabists warned President Bush against the intervention, exactly because it would upset the delicate balance between Sunnis and Shias in Iraq, and that a number of US "concerned IR scholars" organized against what they saw as a dangerous undertaking. Neither should it be forgotten that John Mearsheimer and other realists came out strongly against the intervention, giving as their reason that the United States simply did not need to worry. As he put it in his preferred folksy American idiom, if you are the biggest guy on the block, why stand on the rooftops and shout about it?

To sum up, in the early days of the states system, interventions were about getting between the king and his territory, that is, intervention was a fairly straightforward land grab. With the rise of the idea that there should be some bond between the ruler and his subjects—the idea that evolved into popular sovereignty—intervention became a question of getting between the king and his people. Where formerly intervention was a fairly straightforward land grab, it now became more of a question of what regime type should be lording it over the land in question. There may be a new change in the making, where interventions are framed more as humanitarian interventions, which happen on behalf of an international society. Note, however, that even if interventions are humanitarian and understood as such by a number of parties, they will still be controversial, since humanitarian interventions are not only humanitarian but also interventions, and interventions open the door for all kinds of aboveboard and underhanded politics. Finally, there is John Stuart Mill and his argument in favor of nonintervention: if intervention is about regime change, if the desired regime is underpinned by and depend on a specific kind of social order, and if that order is not in place, then thought should be given to whether outside intervention will help such a social order emerge. The recent record suggests that this question is perhaps in need of rather more thinking than Western politicians have given it so far.

Key Questions

What is the relationship between intervention and sovereignty?

Can interventions be humanitarian?

Notes

1. Culottes were silk knee-breeches and if you dressed without them (sans culottes) and used long trousers instead, you were definitely a piece of lowlife.

2. Civil wars, or situations that a would-be intervening state represents as a civil war, are historically inviting of intervention by a third party; see Little 1975.

3. On specific IR arguments on nonintervention, see Vincent 1974. Note that "intervention" is not used about the process of establishing and maintaining colonies and empires. The temporality of these processes is too slow to allow such usage.

Bibliography

Barbieri, Katherine, and Jack Levy. 1999. "Sleeping with the Enemy: The Impact of War on Trade." *Journal of Peace Research* 36 (4): 463–79.

Barthold, Vasili. V. [1928] 1968. *Turkistan Down to the Mongol Invasion*. London: Gibb Memorial Series.

Finnemore, Martha. 2003. *The Purpose of Intervention*. Ithaca: Cornell University Press.

Little, Richard. 1975. *Intervention: External Involvement in Civil Wars*. Totowa, NJ: Rowman and Littlefield.

John Stuart Mill. [1859] 1973. "A Few Words on Non-Intervention." In *Essays on Politics and Culture*, ed. Gertrude Himmelfarb, 368–84. Gloucester: Peter Smith.

Vincent, John. 1974. *Nonintervention and International Order*. Princeton: Princeton University Press.

19 ✦ Gender, Class, Ethnicity

There is neither Jew nor Greek, there is neither bond nor free,
There is neither male nor female: for ye are all one in Christ Jesus.

KING JAMES BIBLE, GALATIANS 3:28

Humans do not simply record stuff, we actively select what we want to perceive. To put it differently, for each and every individual, the gaze and all the other senses are socially constructed. Furthermore, we often jump to conclusions; if we see a part of something, we picture the whole of which we think it is a part. All this is to say that we categorize reality—categories come before (are anterior to) perception. The more we know about the categories that shape our cognition, the better we perceive. This final chapter is basically about how categorization works and how it impinges on the life chances of individuals who are categorized in this or that way. Such general logics underpin social life on all levels, the international and the global levels included. A particularly muscular example of such a category is caste, an endogamous group of people that tends to congeal around a profession and has a fixed slot in an overarching status hierarchy of castes (Dumont [1966] 1980). Individuals cannot easily escape their caste. When modernity hit India, caste came under attack, but it still permeates life in the subcontinent. To give but one example, personal ads in Hindu newspapers are usually ordered and ranked by caste. In this chapter, however, we are going to look at three other categories, namely gender, class, and ethnicity.

Gender

One key site of contested categorization during the last two centuries has been gender. Gender is the relevant social fact, the presentations of male and female and hybridizations thereof that float about a particular social setting.

Sex is the biological raw material out of which gender is made. As 20th century French feminist Simone de Beauvoir put it, woman is not something one is; it is something one becomes. That's sex understood as gender, as learned social performance. Knowledge production is integral to these contestations. With feminism hitting its stride in the 1970s and '80s, feminists have contributed to most if not all academic disciplines. In medicine, feminists uncovered how much more money is spent on specifically male diseases, and how the typical imagined patient is a male. In archaeology, feminists demonstrated that, among hunters and gatherers, almost all symbolism may turn on the hunt, a typically male preserve, but the overwhelming amount of calories consumed comes from gathering, which is typically gendered female.

Furthermore, on closer historical inspection, it turns out that subject positions such as hunter, pirate, warrior, and so on may be gendered male—social expectations hold that males will do these things—but, in actual fact, we also find women doing them. There is a gap between discourse about how things should be, and practices that determine how they are. Social scientists thrive in and on such interstices. In IR, a key example of a debate along these lines has been the one about war. As noted in chapter 14, in 1987 Jean Bethke Elshtain published *Women and War*, where she made the point that among males, one found the violent many and the pacific few, whereas among women, it was the other way around. Subsequent work has specified our understanding of who does what with which effects during war, and demonstrated the truly varied way in which different societies have gone about their war-making in terms of gender.

Uncovering such dissimilarities presupposes a scientific gaze that focuses on gender, for if we do not draw on the category of gender when we analyze, women's work will often remain hidden. Neither will we be able to uncover differences in life chances that are due to gender (Chappell 2015). Such findings have scientific value in themselves, as they demonstrate how structure, outcome, and life chances follow certain social lines, in this case, gender. In addition, such findings have a political potential for change, as they document variance where things were thought to be invariant, and so demonstrate that things might have been and may be different.

Humans studied may or may not be reflexive about their gender. In many cultures, say in Latin American ones, maleness is seen as biologically anchored and located in the testicles (Sp. *cojones*). Other cultures categorize in a less openly biological fashion. Gender is one of the truly variegated global concepts. "Being a man" entails very different things around the globe. For example, being muscular was not particularly important in Europe in the 18th century. It is important in the United States today, but in Indonesia it is a sign of working-class masculinity. Furthermore, and as demonstrated by this latter example, there is rarely if ever one singular representation of what gender entails. "Manhood" is varied in every social setting, usually due to class differences, but also due to other social variation. Think about tight clothing, or the use of bikinis in public (in Europe and the United States: while it is considered neutral on beaches, it is considered working class in other public settings such as in shopping areas or at car racing). Gender, class, and ethnicity intersect to create what we call subject positions—ready-made identities into which subjects can step. We refer to this interplay of basic social characteristics that result in identities as intersectionality.

Gender changes over time. In his pathbreaking work *Making Sex*, American historian Thomas Laqueur (1990) demonstrated how, during the European Middle Ages and up until the mid-18th century, there was no basic difference between men and women. They both had souls (as per the Church's First Council of Nicaea 325 AD), and they both had toiling bodies. The key difference was that women were weaker: weaker in body, weaker in mind. From the mid-18th century onward, that is, with the onset of modernity, males and females were increasingly seen as qualitatively, as opposed to quantitatively, different. This was new. The effects of this way of seeing things were wide-ranging. First, it meant that the hierarchy between genders went from being quantitatively based to being qualitatively based. The difference went from being a continuum to being binary. Gender became a question of being either man or woman, as opposed to being more or less masculine and feminine. A second effect was that it became harder to cross the line between categories, as it is harder to traverse a binary divide than to slide on a continuum.

Here we have the key reason why everything that has to do with homosexuality, cross-dressing, and transgender is so politically fraught in many settings today, including in relations between states. Such social phenomena, varied manifestations of which are ubiquitous and transhistorical, do not fit the dominant way of classifying the social world. A split between discourse (gender is binary) and practice (gender may be performed in ways that are not clearly marked male/female in discourse) becomes evident. So-called queer theory plays with this. Sedgwick (1993, 8) defines queer as "the open mesh of possibilities, gaps, overlaps, dissonances and resonances, lapses and excesses of meaning when the constituent elements of anyone's gender, of anyone's sexuality aren't made (or can't be made) to signify monolithically." The locus classicus is American literary critic Leslie Fiedler's 1948 essay "Come Back to the Raft Ag'in, Huck Honey," where Fiedler decided to read the novel as if Tom Sawyer and Huckleberry Finn were an item. He "queered" the novel. It took half a century for the first book-length example of this particular reading technique, Cynthia Weber's (1999) queering of American foreign policy, to appear in IR.

A key part of the feminist project is to change the idea that the female is qualitatively different from *and* inferior to males. One important divide between feminists goes between those who maintain the idea of *difference* between genders (e.g., Irigaray 1974) and those who go for *equality*, often understood as sameness. Difference-feminism is present but marginal in Anglo-American tradition. In that tradition, there have been roughly three waves of feminism. The first wave centered on formal democratic rights, voting, and access to state jobs such as that of diplomat (1890s-1940s). In IR, Ann Towns's (2010) work demonstrates how including women first happened in Finland, Norway, New Zealand, and so on, and how this was widely interpreted among the great powers of the day as a sign of lack of civilizational depth. The dominant expectation during modernity was that as civilizations matured, women would be pushed out of leadership positions. The second wave took place in the 1960s and 1970s, when political activism pushed the agenda of social rights. From the 1980s onward, we have seen a third wave. As already noted, the common denominator of the third wave has been an interest in hybridization, that is, in how gender is produced by specific practices that leave loose threads and mess up categorization.

The major interest of gender to social analysis lies in its being a constitutive element of social relations based on perceived differences between the sexes (Scott 1986, 1067). Gender is key to the division of labor. A basic step of analysis is to find out who does what, and one key question to ask here is "where are the women" (Enloe 1989). Once that is established, a second question to ask is what are the hierarchies between different jobs, and how is that hierarchy entangled with gender. This is key to international relations, for everything that has to do with decision making on behalf of groups is tied up with status differentials, simply because taking decisions on behalf of groups is a prestigious thing to do. Gender comes into this in terms of how taking decisions is gendered—to what degree is it considered a masculine thing to do?—and also in terms of personnel. For example, it is a fact that Saudi Arabia as of 2018 has never appointed a female ambassador, and never received one. This tells us something about the gendering of diplomacy.

Gender is absolutely central to social analysis, because gender is always there. Barring the possibility of perpetual cloning, it is impossible to think of a polity where gender is not relevant. Therefore, gender analysis is always a relevant aspect of social analysis. However, gender is not unique in this respect. If polities are defined in terms of we-ness, resources, and hierarchical organization, then there are two other social characteristics that will also be present. These are class (a consequence of hierarchy) and ethnicity (a consequence of we-ness).

Class

If a polity is hierarchical, then the humans that make it up will be hierarchically ordered. We call the different layers of humans in an overarching hierarchy classes. Marx defined them in relation to the means of production: if you own them, you are at the top; if you don't, you are at the bottom; and if there is ambiguity, you are in the middle. More recently, French anthropologist and sociologist Pierre Bourdieu (1930–2002) focused the debate on class by pointing, on the one hand, to *habitus*, by which he meant a distinct way of being in the world (attitude to one's own body, bodily comportment, ways of relating to other humans), and, on the other hand, to *consumption*, that is, what we wear and eat, what cultural artifacts we like, who we spend time with. Bodily comportment and consumption patterns mark individuals as belonging to a class; a social scientist would simply verb the noun class and say that they class them. The resulting divisions and tensions within society are of immense interest to social analysis.

There are two key sequences in international relations where class is key. One are the classical revolutions: American (1776), French (1789), Russian (1917), and Chinese (1949). These were fought in the name of class—the two former against aristocratic class privilege, the two latter against bourgeois class privilege. Let me give you an example of how this categorization scheme had direct and fatal repercussions for individual life chances. When the Bolsheviks ordered their secret police, the Cheka, to initiate the so-called red terror on 2 September 1918, the order contained the following passage:

> We shall not wage war against individuals. We shall exterminate the bourgeoisie as a class. The intelligence work demands that we ask not about blame, but about class. Who are the parents? What is his profession and education? These are the questions that will decide the fate of the accused. (Latsis, quoted in Leggett 1981, 114)

In Bolshevik thinking, class trumped not only the individual, but also the state—with the coming of proletarian rule, the state would wither away, as would, logically, relations between states. Lenin and his comrades seem to have been a wee bit premature on that one (see chapter 4).

In addition to classical revolutions, class is of the essence in discussions about international hierarchy and development. Adolf Hitler, führer of Nazi Germany (1933–45), spoke about proletarian nations, with the basic idea being to transpose class struggle from the domestic arena to the international arena: in the same way as the ownerless proletarians should take over in Germany, ill-treated Germany should get its place in the international sun. In the 1960s, theorists of underdevelopment made a similar move when they stressed, as good neo-Marxists, that class struggle was an international phenomenon. To people like Samir Amin, Andre Gunder Frank, and Johan Galtung, the upper classes in developed and underdeveloped countries had made an alliance against people in what, in parallel to the French idea of the third estate that was discussed in the previous chapter, they called the Third World.[1] Crucially, they saw the working classes in the developed or industrialized world as what, using a Leninist term, they called a labor aristocracy. By this they meant that the rising living standards of Western workers had bought their loyalty, so that they did not show solidarity with workers in the nonindustrialized world, but instead followed their own bourgeoisies. The same basic idea may be found in a rather more tightly theorized form as so-called Gramscian hegemony (Anderson 2017). Hegemony simply means that you are first among equals (see chapter 15). Gramscian hegemony means that everybody, and not only those on top, is happy with this, that the subalterns (those at the receiving end of the hierarchy) have internalized the state of things as natural. A social scientist should always know her subalterns, for their low status makes them both a political joker and a special ethical concern. It would probably be a nice sensitizing exercise to think through who the subalterns in the society you know best are, and to what extent you may recognize them according to the producing and consuming criteria we use to pinpoint class.

Ethnicity

Finally, ethnicity, which comes from Greek *ethnos*—meaning folk (as in folk music), people—and refers to we-ness, and more specifically, the experiencing of being part of that people and being experienced by other members as such. But how? Typical markers of belonging are cultural codes—language, practices, religion—and descent. An ethnicity based on cultural codes we call *civic*—anyone can join if they only master the codes. One example of such ethnicity would be the Proto-Indo-European one that existed in the Eurasian steppe some 6, 000 to 7,000 years ago: if you swore allegiance to a chief and sacrificed to the gods in the proper manner, you were in. By contrast, an ethnicity based on descent we call *primordial*. An example would be Jewishness—if you are not born of a Jewish womb, you have to go through all kinds of extensive training and ritual to fit in, and there will always be those who think you should be denied this, that, or the other thing because your descent is not kosher. Primordial thinking leads invariably to exclusion of others from the "we," and there will always be people to exclude: minorities, neighbors, immigrants, refugees.

In international relations, ethnicity is particularly important because of the doctrine of nationalism, which, as discussed in chapter 8, spells out that all who share an ethnicity make up a nation, and that a nation should have its own state. Like class, ethnicity can be turned into an ordering principle of international society. There is a sense in which 19th and early 20th century European history may be read as a struggle between these two principles, with the hard left trying to organize the social according to class, and the hard right trying to organize it according to ethnicity. The outbreak of the First World War gave us the answer: most people everywhere, and that includes people like the father of Russian Marxism, Georgi Plekhanov, identified with nation over class. With the demise of the Soviet Union in 1991 and Yugoslavia in 1992, we can conclude that the hard right won everywhere: it is still the case that ethnicity trumps class as a basic principle of political organization.

One last question: What kind of ontic status should we assign to these three basic social categories of gender, class, and ethnicity? The traditional answer is biology. Aristotle held that class differences went back to there being natural slaves among humans. Sigmund Freud held that sex is destiny, by which he presumably meant that biology couldn't be trumped by the social. A century later, that seems a strange view. A social scientist who reads about Freud's women patients would ask if they were "hysterical" because of their wombs, that is, because of some physiological factor as suggested by the term's etymology (from Gr. *hysteresis*, womb), or because of some fluke in their psychological makeup, as Freud thought, or whether there was something about the social situation that made for a structural holding back of women, which led to frustration that in some cases resulted in mental illness. As social scientists, we privilege the social factors, and we try to explain social phenomena in terms of other social phenomena. That, however, should not blind us to the importance of physiology and psychology, for physiology and psychology lie down the bandwidths inside which social variation is possible.

My own view is that the self, no matter if that is an individual or a collective self like a polity, is narrated. We tell narratives about who we are. We omit stuff that actually happened, we add stuff that has not happened, we edit stuff and rearrange its relevance, and we fight for narratives about who we are so that we may have them recognized by others. American literary critic Kenneth Burke ([1945] 1969) sees narratives as consisting of five elements: act (what is going on), scene (where and when in social and physical space is it going on), agent (who acts), agency (by dint of what do they act), and purpose (reasons and motives for acting). So, on the one hand, there is what we may call a base or an inventory of elements that are there: gender depends on sex; class depends on patterns of relationships to production and consumption; ethnicity depends on common perceived descent and mastery of cultural codes such as language. Some of these elements, like sex and skin color, are harder to change than others (but the *relevance* of these elements may always be changed). Anthropologist Ernest Gellner called these entropy-resistant. But, on the other hand, these elements may be used to tell different narratives. Is it the case that someone who works outside the home must be a man? That someone who buys their own furniture may be upper middle class? That an ethnically non-English person may be mayor of London? And so on, and so forth. Marx captured this duality where class was concerned by talking about class as an analytical category on the one hand, and class as lived consciousness on the other. When Marx wrote that peasants are a sack of potatoes, he wanted to pinpoint how peasants are not able to act as a class because they do not experience themselves as a class. Marxists often talk about the need to "raise class consciousness," by which they mean turn what *they* think is a class by *their* analytical lights into class as a lived and self-reflexive reality experienced by those *they* think should make it up. Any political project will by definition include a conceptual component, for defining concepts in specific ways is a way of defining social reality, and defining social reality is one of the goals of politics. By contrast, when judged as a scientific project, this kind of mixing up of analytical categories that we use to understand social reality, on the one hand, and the categories that the people studied live by, on the other, is a recipe for bad analysis. If we do not keep clear distinctions between analytical and what we may call hermeneutical concepts and are not clear about when we talk about what, our analyses will necessarily suffer.

There is an ongoing struggle not only about how relevant to political life certain identities based on gender, class, and ethnicity should be (as when certain American Republicans tout the importance of reaching what they refer to as a color-blind society or certain feminists argue that gender is an "imperative status," that is, always dominant), but also about what being a man, a bourgeois, a Norwegian means. To end on a repeated quote, when Simone de Beauvoir wrote about gender that a woman is not something you are, but something you become, she was also making a general point, namely that categories are emergent, in the sense that they are always in a process of renewal and change. We may analyze how categories change by analyzing how the categories that define them are always contested. Given that we may see entire societies and states, as well as the relations between them, as defined by categorization, we have in the analysis of concepts a key to understanding the social world at large.

Key Questions

Is the state gendered?

Can political analysis do away with social categories?

Note

1. The Third World was the nonindustrial opposite of the Western First World (industrialized by capitalism) and the Soviet Second World (industrialized by com-

munism). As the Second World disappeared with the fall of the Soviet Union and its East European empire in 1989–91, the Third World also disappeared and the Global South took its place.

Bibliography

Anderson, Perry. 2017. *The H-Word: The Peripeteia of Hegemony*. London: Verso.

Burke, Kenneth. [1945] 1969. *A Grammar of Motives*. Berkeley: University of California Press.

Chappell, Louise. 2015. *The Politics of Gender Justice at the International Criminal Court*. Oxford: Oxford University Press.

Cotter, David A., Joan M. Hermsen, Seth Ovadia, and Reeve Vanneman. 2001. "The Glass Ceiling Effect." *Social Forces* 80 (2): 655–81.

Dumont, Louis. [1966] 1980. *Homo Hierarchicus: The Caste System and Its Implications*. Chicago: University of Chicago Press.

Elshtain, Jean Bethke. 1987. *Women and War*. Brighton: Harvester Press.

Enloe, Cynthia. 1989. *Bananas, Beaches and Bases: Making Feminist Sense of International Politics*. London: Pandora.

Irigaray, Luce. 1974. *Speculum of the Other Woman*. Ithaca: Cornell University Press.

Laqueur, Thomas W. 1990. *Making Sex: Body and Gender from the Greeks to Freud*. Cambridge: Harvard University Press.

Leggett, George. 1981. *The Cheka: Lenin's Political Police*. Oxford: Clarendon.

Putnam, Robert D. 1976. *The Comparative Study of Political Elites*. Englewood Cliffs, NJ: Prentice-Hall.

Scott, Joan. 1986. "Gender: A Useful Category of Historical Analysis." *American History Review* 91 (5): 1053–75.

Sedgwick, Eve Kosofsky. 1993. *Tendencies*. Durham, NC: Duke University Press.

Towns, Ann. 2010. *Women and States: Norms and Hierarchies in International Society*. Cambridge: Cambridge University Press.

Weber, Cynthia. 1999. *Faking It: US Hegemony in a "Post-Phallic" Era*. Minneapolis: University of Minnesota Press.

A Note on the Author

Iver B. Neumann is Director of Norwegian Social Research (NOVA) at Oslo Metropolitan University and Adjunct Professor at the Museum of Cultural History, University of Oslo. He holds doctorates in Politics (Oxford, 1992) and Social Anthropology (Oslo, 2009). He was Montague Burton Professor at the London School of Economics, 2012–17, Director of Research at the Norwegian Institute of International Affairs, 2010–11, and Professor in Russian Studies at the University of Oslo, 2006–9. He contributed to the building up of an International Relations program as Adjunct Professor at the Norwegian University of Life Sciences, 2010–12. Among his 20 books are *Russia and the Idea of Europe* (2nd ed., 2017), *Uses of the Other: "The East" in European State Formation* (1999), *Governing the Global Polity* (with Ole Jacob Sending, University of Michigan Press, 2010), *At Home with the Diplomats: Inside a European Ministry of Foreign Affairs* (2012), *Diplomatic Sites* (2013), and (with Einar Wigen) *The Eurasian Steppe Tradition in International Relations, 4000 BCE–2018 CE: Russia, Turkey and European State Building* (2018).

Index

Note: Page numbers in italics refer to figures and tables.